SHADOWS of EMOTIONS

SHADOWS of EMOTIONS

Life after the dream

KEVIN IJA BARNETT, SR.

Copyright © 2020 by Kevin IJA Barnett, Sr.

All rights reserved. This book or any portion thereof may not be reproduced or used in any manner whatsoever without the express written permission of the author except for the use of brief quotations in a book review.

ISBN: 978-0-578-65363-1

happyselfpublisher.com

To Muriel and Lois, my two moms

TABLE OF CONTENTS

Still In The Shadows 1
    NO PEACHES AND CREAM 4
    LIGHT IN THE DARKNESS 7
Seeking Closure 11
    THE PAIN OF OLD LOST DREAMS 12
    CLOSING THE BOOK ON A DREAM 20
Guilt 25
    SHADOWS OF NEW GUILT 27
    SHADOWS OF OLD GUILT 31
    THE VICTIM MENTALITY 33
Anger 39
    FAMILY BATTLES 42
    TOOLS FOR BATTLE 47
Depression 53
    DEPRESSION BLUES 55

    WARNING SIGNS 58

Joy 63

    FINDING FEAR IN JOY 67

    A JOY LIKE NO OTHER 70

    JOY FUELS THE JOURNEY 74

Hope 77

    DEEPER HOPES 81

    HOPE CHANGES 84

    SWIMMING IN HOPE 88

Rejection 91

    REJECTION AT MY DOORSTEP 93

    LIVING IN REJECTION MODE 95

    REJECTION PAYBACK 97

    REJECTION STRATEGIES 99

Peace 105

    LOSING FAMILY, FINDING PEACE 106

    THE GREATEST PEACE OF ALL 111

The "Why?" Questions 113

    THE HOLE THAT NEEDS FILLING 114

- SEEKING TO FILL THE HOLE 118
- ACCEPTING THE QUESTIONS WITHOUT ANSWERS 121

Love 125
- THE INSTILLING OF LOVE 128
- THE DEATH OF LOVE 131
- THE MIRACLE OF LOVE 133

Regret 139
- LIVING IN THE PAST 140
- THE REALITY OF REGRET 146
- HEALING FROM REGRET 148

Released From the Shadows 153
IN GRATITUDE 163
CONTACT 167
ABOUT THE AUTHOR 169

I was 37 years old.

I didn't know who my birth parents were.

I didn't know if I had any brothers or sisters.

Those questions burned a hole inside of me.

I had wandered, like Moses, in the wilderness, on a quest to search for the family I had lost.

The family I had never known.

I knew I had to get to a better place, to finally answer the question:

"Who am I?"

God was giving me a chance, to come out of my shadows.

The waiting was over.

No more feeling helpless.

No more believing it was impossible.

No more letting the past put chains around my future.

And no more living in the shadows.

Now was the time.

FROM:

Living My Shadows: Dreams Do Come True

INTRODUCTION

Still In The Shadows

No mother. No father. No sisters. No brothers.

No future. No past. No roots. No home.

I was a shadow nobody wanted from the start.

Those words, from my first book *Living My Shadows: Dreams Do Come True*, summed up the first 56 years of my life.

I had been abandoned at birth by my mother. My first foster parents raised me for a year, then wrapped me in a blanket and left me on a stranger's front porch, never to be seen again. The truth about my birth family was locked up and kept secret. I had no clue who I was, or where I came from. For 56 years, I saw myself as an unwanted child, abused and tormented, cast into the shadows.

Being abandoned colored my days and haunted my nights. People told me I would never find my bloodline. No matter how hard I pushed, no matter how deep I dug, finding my birth family would elude me, they said. Yet on September 17, 2016, at a soul food restaurant in Asbury Park, I was reunited with my birth mother, and my brother and sister. Months later, I'd met a host of cousins and blood relatives, learned the identity of my father, and celebrated my 57th birthday with my Mom singing happy birthday to me.

My chase had come full circle. Where my life had once taken a dark turn, a light now appeared. After living a life of secrets, I was living my dream.

Life has changed a lot since my dreams came true in 2016. I've overcome the cruel circumstances of my birth, and reunited my

SHADOWS OF EMOTIONS

family on both sides, bringing the family triad—birth mom/birth father/adopted parents—together.

After 2016, I didn't think my life could get much better. I thought all the old feelings I'd once experienced—the pain of abandonment, the confusion of living in foster homes, the constant fear of being whipped and beaten—were gone forever.

I never expected new feelings of hurt, resentment, and anger to rise up in their place.

I didn't expect my feelings, my emotions to cast me back into the shadows.

Clawing myself out of those shadows was why I wrote my first book. I wanted to help others like myself—lost children on the hunt for their biological families—claw their way out, too.

The first part of my story has been told now. But there's more to my story. My story isn't finished. Not by a long shot.

KEVIN IJA BARNETT, SR.

NO PEACHES AND CREAM

After tracking down my biological family, I was certain everything in my life would be peaches and cream. I'd ride off into the sunset, waving goodbye to the painful past, and be happy.

I quickly discovered that's not the case. Suddenly I was filled with stress, with fear and anxiety—anxiety because I now had three families to worry about.

I had my mother's side of the family to worry about. I had my father's side to worry about. I also had my adopted family to worry about.

This was all new terrain for me. Because of the fear and anxiety those new worries gave birth to, I found myself living in the shadows again.

But these were different shadows. These were the shadows of feelings, the shadows of emotions. New emotions, given weight by the same old ones.

I found myself having to juggle how I spent my time. Was I neglecting my adopted family? Was I spending too much time with my birth family—or not spending enough time with them? And what about my wife, and our family? Was I ignoring them? When my wife met me, it was just the two of us and my adopted family. Now, it's me and my biological relatives—cousins, aunts, uncles, some from as far away as Africa, some from the Caribbean, some from the Virgin Islands. It's an extra 600 people we're having to juggle!

How would I channel all these new needs? I had no clue. Then there was the emotional challenge of putting my story into print.

Once my first book was published, I started going out and having book signings. I had book signings in my hometown, book signings in libraries, book signings down at the beach. I started a small business called Living My Shadows LLC, through which I was engaged in motivational speaking.

Sharing my story was thrilling. It transformed my life. The groups I spoke to were shocked. Like myself, many were adoptees, or had been in the foster care system, and lived through that emotional rollercoaster, feeling hopeless and sorry for themselves. Hearing my journey to finding my parents illuminated a path they could follow. Many couldn't believe I was able to overcome the pain and rage I'd once felt, and still not carry a lot of hatred in my heart.

There was a great sense of fulfillment, in being able to help these individuals overcome their own obstacles. Yet each time I spoke, I had to relive the old suffering, the pain, the heartbreak. I had to relive the abuse, the torture, the stress of life beating me down. I had to look those emotions in the eye, and not let those old shadows swallow me again.

SHADOWS OF EMOTIONS

Book One was the proof I could persevere and overcome my previous messed-up life. Yet walking the path after Book One created new holes in my heart, new hardships, new emotional shadows.

LIGHT IN THE DARKNESS

Book Two, *Shadows of Emotions*, is the story of how I clawed my way out of these new emotional shadows.

Book Two was written to prepare others taking my same journey for the emotional, physical and spiritual shadows they will face.

In many ways, I will always be living those shadows. There are days when I look back at my life and feel like I'm 56 years behind the curve. I feel like if I live to be 112—which is 56 more years from the time I wrote my first book—I will still feel cheated like I only lived half a life.

Shadows of Emotions is my battle to overcome that lie. It's me facing reality. Facing my new fears. Facing those new emotions, and kicking that victim mentality in the butt.

It's the story of how I motivated myself to be unstoppable in beating the odds. How I became stronger, gained clarity, and tapped into my faith to continue the journey. In telling my story, I hope to show you the path to courage, to help you get past whatever wall you can't seem to climb.

Writing *Shadows of Emotions* has been my therapy.

My hope is that reading this book will be your therapy, too.

I hope this book helps you find hope, healing, and closure.

Even with the miracle of finding my birth parents and my bloodline, I still find myself seeking closure. Some days, I'm not even sure what closure would look like.

There are some answers I will never get. There is time lost I will never catch up on. There are too many family secrets, too many questions, and too many painful moments I wish I could rewrite.

Closure is elusive. Yet closure is that voice that keeps speaking to me. Closure is the missing part of my story, the story that remains untold. Closure is that light shining in the darkness.

I hope this book will be that light shining in the darkness for you. Let's talk more about the concept of closure, and the emotions we all need to battle through, in the next chapter.

CHAPTER ONE

Seeking Closure

Why do we need closure? Why do you and I seek to "let go" and come to terms with things that happened long ago? What do we hope to gain by trying to heal the past, by writing THE END on a chapter in our lives? And why do we need closure to move on from a relationship, an emotional hurt, or a personal trauma?

According to the dictionary, the word closure means "finality; a letting go of what once was."

Closure is all about letting go. It's about releasing that old trauma, those old questions, that old pain.

Letting go is how we accept that we've done all we can to heal the past and that we're ready to move forward with our life. Closure gives us a sense of peace, a sense of resolution. It gives us a feeling of control, where we didn't feel in control anymore.

When I completed writing Book One, *Living My Shadows*, I thought for certain I'd found closure. I'd tracked down my birth family. I'd reunited with my birth mom, my siblings, and my bloodline. I'd found the answers I was seeking for more than 50 years, and that gave me a feeling of peace. That gave me serenity.

But that peace and serenity only lasted a moment. Because closure is elusive.

THE PAIN OF OLD LOST DREAMS

Two years later, the meaning of closure has changed for me. My emotional need for closure has changed. And I've found it's hard to move on, to move forward, when you're still looking for answers, when you're still haunted

SHADOWS OF EMOTIONS

by the past, reliving old traumas, trying to bust down walls that have been built up all around you.

To find closure, we must first contend with disappointment, anger, hurt, and the pain of old lost dreams.

After finishing my first book, and seeing it published, I experienced a deep sense of relief and a feeling of accomplishment. I'd found the answer to the question that had hounded and haunted me my whole life: Who am I? I'd completed the task I had set out to do: find my bloodline. And by writing my book, I'd shared my story with others like myself—adoptees and orphans who were still seeking those answers, still wanting that closure, who could learn from the mistakes I'd made and the triumphs I'd experienced and blaze their own path.

As I went out to do motivational speaking engagements and book signings on behalf of the book, I felt a great weight had been lifted from my shoulders. But I also felt a new weight had been added.

It was the weight of all those folks in the past who'd told me I'd fail, and all the old scars I still carried from pursuing my dreams.

Mind you, I had the full support of my family. My birth family and my adoptive family were fully on board, accepting my need for closure, for answers, pushing me to get my story out and help heal others who were on my same journey. I had the sweet relief of knowing they were on my side.

Still, I had doubts. There were times when I felt insecure, because I was stepping into new relationships, and uncertain how I'd handle these new emotions.

My first speaking engagement was when I realized chasing closure would bring a new round of suffering.

My first book signing was at a church function, at the Citadel of Hope Mission in New Jersey. It was Founder's Day, and the church allowed my book to be part of the celebration. As soon as my story got out, there was a multitude of different reactions. A lot of people already knew I was adopted but didn't know the full story of my trauma—the abuse and neglect of my foster parents—and how my birth family and I were reunited. The reaction to my book was divided. Some people were astonished. Some were inspired, shaking my hand and slapping me on the back, and telling me, "Oh wow, this is great, you found your family!" Some were shocked at the violence that had been perpetrated against me as a child, in the foster care system. The cruelty I spoke about in my book shook them to their very core.

Telling my story in the book had shaken me. Going back through those old moments sometimes felt like being in bondage, like I'd survived walking through an inferno, and was now stepping back into it.

My adoptive family, as well as my sister and brother, came to Delaware to be part of my second book signing. We brought the entire family together, for a cookout. My emotions soared; my feelings couldn't have been higher. It was so uplifting, so encouraging, so motivating to see my entire bloodline gathered around me and to hear stories of how my book had affected people, in a positive way.

For a long time, the emotional downs I'd felt along the way to writing my book faded into the past. All that was behind me now. I thought it would stay that way.

I was on a high for a long time. Doing a lot of book signings, answering questions from other adoptees on Facebook, starting up my motivational speaking business. Publishing the book had launched everything, as well as giving me a sense of who I am. It was cleansing, to finally share my story. It was therapy. It helped me deal with my old feelings of being abandoned by my family. Telling my story in the book, and knowing it was inspiring others to deal with their own issues, was the icing on the cake.

Or so I thought.

Because through all the emotional highs of getting my story out, the need for emotional closure kept speaking to me. And kept haunting me. And the lack of closure brought me crashing back down to earth.

As the next two years passed, that initial feeling that I was living my dream slowly but surely evaporated. I was rocked by deaths in the family. My nephew was murdered. A cousin I'd recently met passed away. Then my aunt—my mother's sister who'd help support me when I was in the foster care system—also passed away. So I began experiencing death in the family, which I hadn't experienced in that way before. With each death, the chance to create a new relationship or for closure in that relationship was abruptly cut short.

Along with this new experience of death, came a new feeling: guilt. I began feeling guilty.

KEVIN IJA BARNETT, SR.

I felt guilty that I hadn't spent enough time with my new family. Because I was now divvying up my time between family members, I began neglecting the family that raised me. I was spending a lot of time with my biological mother, in Asbury, trying to catch up on lost time. At the same time as I was doing this, I felt indirectly like I was neglecting the rest of my family.

These feelings of guilt increased. I felt guilty now for wanting closure. I felt guilty for seeking answers, and suddenly having to deal with the questions that would never be answered.

As I started learning more and more about my late father and visiting his graveside, I began feeling another emotion: anger. I was angry because I'd never seen my father, never met him, never shaken his hand or felt him embrace me in a hug. I was angry because I felt my mother was responsible for keeping him a secret. Then I was angry that I didn't get a chance to see my brother Kenny, who'd passed away in the 1990s.

Sometimes I'd get so angry, thinking about these things, that my hands would shake.

The more I sought closure, the more my anger kicked in. When I attended the funeral of a cousin, all of a sudden I found people coming up to me, thinking I was my brother Kenny. It was weird. "Oh, Kenny," they told me, "I thought you'd passed away!" At the time, I shrugged it off. But as time passed, and I'd replay those dreams in my head of someday meeting my blood brother, the disappointment I now felt broke my heart. The longer that heartbreak lingered, the angrier I became.

Dealing with all this anger, at the same time as I was losing members of my new family, wasn't just hard. It was excruciating.

It was during this time that I sensed my adopted family was going through similar feelings. I could sense that they suddenly felt scared. My adopted baby brother and my adopted father both asked, "Are you going to leave us? Are you going to forget?" Leave you? I thought. Why would you think that? That broke my heart. I vowed that I wouldn't—we had such a close-knit bond, and we loved each other dearly. I knew my adopted brother would always be my sibling. I reassured my brother and father that nothing would ever replace them. "I'm just trying to add to my legacy," I explained, "so that my kids understand where they come from, what their bloodline is," I explained about wanting to know the medical history of my blood family.

But the need for closure kept speaking to me.

CLOSING THE BOOK ON A DREAM

The original purpose of me finding my birth family was not to find closure—it was to know where I came from, who I really was. In the beginning, I thought there might be a 50/50 chance that I'd ever have a relationship with my birth mother and father, with my blood siblings. If not, if that day never came, I figured I was emotionally prepared. I was ready to deal with that disappointment.

Yet the truth is, I wasn't prepared. Suddenly, I was faced with the reality of having a future with them, of finding the answers to the lifelong questions I'd battled and struggled with, and having to deal with those answers. Suddenly there was the potential for so much more from these relationships than I'd ever dreamed—and not just the good things I'd dreamed of, but the new wounds I'd opened from learning hard truths.

Along with the potential for new wounds came the reality of experiencing even deeper, more difficult emotions. I had a spiderweb of emotions from all sides, from all angles—guilt, anger, disappointment—to deal with now.

I'd closed the book on one dream: finding my family. I'd been accepted by my new family, and I'd accepted each of them. I'd let go of what once was—the emotional baggage of all my old hurt—only to find I now yearned for closure from all these new feelings.

There are things I'll never receive closure for, I now realize. Closure, I'm realizing, is a process, an ongoing thing.

But is finding closure the best thing for us? Does closure give us a sense of false security? Does it give us false hope that we'll no longer be hounded and tormented by these emotions?

And how do we battle through these emotions? How do we move on from the hurt? How do we heal, without closure?

And what do we do, while we're waiting for closure?

I believe we need to give ourselves time to come to a closure. In this microwave culture we live in, we expect everything to come instantly. Closure's not like that. We need time—time to process our feelings, time to accept the new, time to grieve the old. To grieve the loss.

SHADOWS OF EMOTIONS

To forgive, and truly heal. How long this takes is going to be different for each one of us.

As we grieve, we need also to point our vision to the future. We need to look ahead, to make plans to move into new relationships, to let go of those old wounds, to let go of the past.

Finally, we need to stop worrying about closure. We don't need closure, to heal. What we need is a strong foundation to walk forward on. The past is the past. It only exists in our minds. We can't change it. The future is the only place we can make changes.

As I said, closure is elusive. We can't find closure without breaking the shackles of old pain. Closure is all about releasing that old pain, those old hurts, and starting over. Then it's about looking at the world through new eyes, through a new lens.

Writing my first book was like looking at my life through a new lens. Other emotions raised their heads when I started writing this second book. Let's talk about one of them, in Chapter Two.

CHAPTER TWO

Guilt

Trying to control our emotions is a constant battle, an everyday struggle. We've all been there. We try to run from some emotions; some we welcome in like a long-lost family member; some pound us with pain and make our heart race, and some we savor and celebrate.

We've talked about closure, and a few strategies for achieving closure in our lives. Now let's talk about an emotion that whispers in our heads and tries to dictate our future by reminding us of our past.

Guilt.

KEVIN IJA BARNETT, SR.

A lot of my personal story is connected to guilt. Old hurts. Old pain. Old abuse. Old sadness. Old suffering. Old disappointments. Old failures.

Guilt has been a major player in my life. Though I've fought through it the best I could, there were times when I couldn't tell if guilt was hurting me or healing me. Sometimes my feelings of guilt humiliated me so much that my brain shut down; other times, guilt humbled me to rise up strong and do better.

Guilt is a part of life I've learned to accept. But what does guilt actually feel like?

It's nearly impossible to describe guilt. To me, guilt is like being hungry. You see food in front of you, but it's not the food you want. So you push that food away. You shove it to the side. You still feel hungry, you feel empty, but even if the food is right in front of you, you can't fill that emptiness. Then suddenly that food is gone. It's vanished. In your mind, you question the bad choice you just made. Now there's an emptiness that can never be filled. You could have filled that emptiness, but you didn't. You chose not to. You know you should have done better. And that emptiness nags at you, and gnaws at you, like a never-ending hunger pang, and it never goes away.

Guilt is like getting punched in the gut and watching the video footage of that gut-punch over and over, like a broken record that just keeps skipping.

You probably have your own guilt examples, your own guilt feelings, your own guilt stories.

Here are some of mine.

SHADOWS OF NEW GUILT

As the first months after finding my bloodline passed, I noticed a change in my behavior. I began to feel deep guilt, and anguish, when my thoughts came to my adopted family, the Barnetts.

It might sound crazy, but for some reason, I felt guilty that I'd finally found my bloodline. In my head, I was thinking: Kevin, you better be careful. Your adopted family might think you're pushing them to the side. That they're no longer important in your life. Now, I knew that wasn't true—in fact, I made certain that my adopted father and my brothers knew that wasn't the case. Yet when I'd go visit my birth mother or my birth sister, I'd have these pangs of guilt. I feel like I'm trying to make up for lost time, I thought to myself. I feel guilty for finding my bloodline, for spending time with them, for loving them. I even feel guilty for finally knowing the answer to the question of who I am, and where I come from.

Was I neglecting my adopted family? Indirectly, maybe I was. Did that mean I didn't love them, didn't still care about them, or need them in my life? Of course not! Yet I developed this guilt, these negative shadows of old feelings, and these feelings became an obsession.

Pretty soon, my obsession turned negative in my daily life. Guilt began showing up in new places.

I felt guilty that I was neglecting my own kids. I felt insecure as a father; I knew I wasn't the best father that I could have been, that my sons and daughter were going through things and I wasn't always there for them. This crushed my heart to dust. I'd been so embroiled in my search, and now in getting to know my new family, that I'd neglected my immediate family, my children, my blood kin.

I worried that my obsession would affect my kids, in negative ways. Was the way I'd been treated as a child in foster care, before my adoption, coloring the way I fathered my own children? Try as I might not to blame myself for the past, what had once been missing from my life began to take up more and more precious time in the present. I had a right and every excuse in the world for wanting to connect with my new family.

But still, I felt guilty.

I also felt guilty when it came to expressing my emotions, my feelings. It took me a long time to become comfortable in expressing my feelings, especially when it came to the most important emotion of all:

Love.

Growing up in the foster care system, I wasn't shown, love. I was shown love through my adoptive parents, but the hurt and suffering, the beatings and abuse from those early years in foster care scarred me and caused me to shut my emotions down. Even with my adoptive parents, the Barnetts, it took me a long time to tell my mother and father that I loved them.

Hardness in my heart clouded my head. It affected my relationship with my children, my adopted parents, my bloodline, with everyone. I knew a transformation would have to come, to enable me to express these feelings. Everything in my new life with my blood family was preparation for this change.

SHADOWS OF OLD GUILT

I also experienced guilt from my distant past, the hurt from long ago.

These old guilt feelings were a combination of grief and anger. The feelings were overwhelming and confusing.

I'd think about my old shadows—the Crawfords, for instance, into whose home I'd been placed as a child, then abused, tortured and treated like a slave. I'd feel guilty for thinking they were bad people, for not forgiving them, for hating them.

I felt guilty for my early days as a father—for not being there physically for my boys because I was so bent on trying to make a better life for them financially. I felt guilty for divorcing their mom. I felt guilty for failing them when they were small.

KEVIN IJA BARNETT, SR.

Some of my guilt came from my birth story—from being abandoned, as a baby. Because of that, I didn't want anybody to feel sorry for me. I wanted to prove to the world, and to myself, that I could succeed on my own terms. And because I chased that dream, in order to escape those abandonment issues, that rejection, the guilt of knowing I'd abandoned others in the pursuit of my bloodline followed me everywhere like an angry shadow.

I also experienced guilt for leaving home at a young age. I left home because I yearned to find out who I was. Growing up, there were times I didn't feel I was part of the Barnett family, no matter how well they loved me. I had no idea who I was. I had no photos of myself, from the age of 10 on down. So I felt guilty about leaving home and joining the military. It was the way I did it that bothered me—just leaving home, at age 19, right after high school, without telling anybody, just a note on my dresser telling them I was gone.

Fortunately, I never felt anything negative coming from my adopted family. All the guilt and the negative feelings were bred within me. In fact, my family supported me—they saw I wanted to do this, needed to do this. Even my father, whose heart was aching because of my departure, never said anything to make me feel guilty.

I have always been thankful for that. Luckily, my adopted family knew my heart wasn't in abandoning them. They understood I wasn't trying to replace them.

THE VICTIM MENTALITY

If you're adopted, you know what I'm talking about. A lot of folks who are adopted experience those feelings of rejection, of feeling unwanted, invisible. People who aren't adopted don't usually understand.

I try to explain it to them like this: "When you look in the mirror," I say, "who do you see? When you visit the doctor for a medical exam, and the doctor asks about your family's medical history, what do you say? You probably tell them about your mother and father, your grandmother and grandfather. That's who you have when you look in the mirror."

I tell them, "Those things you have, I don't. That information you take for granted, I've had to hunt and search for, I've had to hope and pray I'd find, my entire life."

Eventually, all the hopelessly hoping and unanswered prayers create a victim mentality. We start to feel and act like a victim, driven by the power of our negative thoughts, our abandonment, our rejection.

The other end of all that hunting and searching and hoping and praying is the anger we feel because the journey has been such a struggle. Starting life at zero is a mindset that puts a chip on your shoulder, a chip that grows even larger the more obstacles and hurdles life throws at you.

SHADOWS OF EMOTIONS

Over time, that chip becomes anger. Next thing we know, we feel guilty for having all that anger.

I speak on this from experience. Voicing my anger and outrage fills me with guilt. That causes me to shut down. When I feel guilty, rather than allowing myself to go into anger—because I know I will go there—I just shut it down, until I feel nothing.

Until I'm numb.

That numbness is the emptiness I was talking about earlier. Feeling nothing, feeling numb, is my control. Once I have that control, I look for an outlet, to release my guilt and anger.

Sometimes my outlet is playing video games. Sometimes it's working out. Sometimes I call my mom or my sister. I go on Facebook, to one of the adoption groups, to see if there's somebody I can help. Through my words, through my experience, I help others, I heal. I release.

Earlier in my life, I would have put up walls. But you can't put up walls, to heal from that pain. You need to have some kind of outlet, to release that pain. You redirect your mindset to something else, to something positive, while you ride the anger out.

Once I stop running from my anger and release it, those old wounds and pain have no power over me.

That's how I've learned to deal with it. I evaluate my guilt feelings, then put them in the proper place, before they turn to anger. And eventually, given time, those feelings of guilt start to fade.

And over time, they go away.

Releasing anger and guilt can be difficult, at times. But I guess life itself is difficult.

All these emotions are tangled up together, like the spider's web we've talked about. They're all connected. Anger is connected with guilt. Guilt is connected with seeking closure. Sometimes, they hit you all at the same time. You feel angry because you feel guilty; you feel guilty because you're angry. This can lead to anxiety, depression, and even destructive behavior.

Guilt requires forgiveness. Otherwise, it never goes away. It comes and goes in circles. As does the next emotion we're going to talk about.

CHAPTER THREE

Anger

Let's make no bones about it: Anger is a condition that every man, woman, and child on earth faces. In fact, it's unimaginable to think of anybody going through life without experiencing the emotion of anger.

Anger relies heavily on negative emotions—emotions like dissatisfaction, discontent, unhappiness, and aggravation.

Is there any greater destructive force on earth than anger? Anger has caused wars. Wars have caused the destruction of whole cities and countries and created famine. Even in our own neighborhoods, anger is responsible for all kinds of violent crime: murder, assault, rape, and mass shootings, to name a few.

As we said in our last chapter, anger often shares a deep connection with feelings of guilt. In guilt, we're no longer living in the present—we're re-experiencing painful memories of the past, and projecting them into the future. In essence, the future no longer exists; we've made up our minds about what will happen in the future, based upon the evidence of where what and who we've failed in the past. Based upon our past failures, we're plagued with guilt, certain we'll fail again. And that we'll continue to fail, again and again.

But anger's not just connected with guilt. Its connection runs deep into pretty much every emotion we can think of. Depression. Rejection. Regret. You name it, and anger is often the thread.

When it comes to anger issues and family, the web of emotions gets even more tangled, and trickier to navigate—to the point of being downright dangerous. Anger can turn instantly to rage, then to hatred. Hatred can quickly turn to acts of violence—even violence against our most loved family members.

Sounds illogical, doesn't it? That those we love deepest can also be the objects of our greatest wrath and even vengeful fury?

Anger and love seem at odds with each other, logic tells us, which is why anger in a family if allowed to take root, to run rampant, can lead to immense suffering and immeasurable pain—pain that sometimes lasts not just for days or weeks, but for years, even generations.

Family anger can run deep, and lead to the destruction of our most cherished relationships. Among those of us seeking to be reunited with their birth family, as I was, anger at the past can overtake our dreams for the future. It can cause us to destroy and throw away the blood relationships we desperately seek.

Anger can wreak havoc, can wreck and ruin our hopes. And it can trip up our dreams when it comes to reconnecting with lost family.

FAMILY BATTLES

I don't know about you. But my greatest anger seems to come from dwelling in negative thoughts about my past, my lost opportunities, and my family.

I'll get angry around birthdays. Thinking about my older brother, I start experiencing animosity toward my birth mother, indignation, even outrage. My mind wanders to all the things I missed with my brother since he passed away early.

From what I hear, my brother and I were similar in so many ways. He wanted to (as we call it) "get out of the 'hood"—meaning Asbury Park—so he joined the military. I did the same. He was independent, leaving home to move to Philly.

SHADOWS OF EMOTIONS

I see so many parallels in our lives. What's missing though in his story are the intimate details, the everyday personal things—things like I never hugged my brother, I never shook his hand. Things like I don't know what he smelled like. Little things that you know growing up about your brother.

So I get angry when birthdays roll around because I missed all the other birthdays of my siblings. Sometimes just looking at old photographs makes me angry. I still have so many unanswered questions—questions about the gaps in my story, about my ancestors, even about my health. I wonder why my mom wasn't there, looking out for me. Why was she so selfish? Yet I know she had her reasons—she only desired my safety, my comfort.

I try not to stay angry too much. Being angry brings on health issues. When I start stressing, I get headaches. All the fears and insecurities I've bottled up all these years start raining down. Buried under all that suffering only makes me angrier and angrier.

It's not just my mom though. I get angry with my father, too.

The reality is I don't know the full story—supposedly he came by the house when I wasn't home. He sat in the same house that I walked through. I wish I could have at least shaken his hand or looked into his eyes. But I was robbed of that. I don't know if that was his way of saving me from pain, of not destroying life with my adoptive family, but I feel like I was owed that.

Another area of anger is with my situation. The scars of my past—both metaphorical and physical scars.

Anger rises every time I look at my body, at my feet and my ankles. Every time I look at those childhood scars I think how close to death I came. I'm upset with my mother because she allowed that to happen—she allowed me to go into the foster care system, where I could be tortured and abused. Those marks on my body remind me of the terror I experienced as a child. They're daily reminders of the horrors I've been through, what I've survived, what I've battled against, what I've overcome.

There are so many angles, so many aspects to my anger.

Sometimes just looking in the mirror fills me with anger.

I'll think about my mother and wonder why she abandoned me. I'll think about the opportunity she had to meet her son when I was an adult, yet she said, "No." What mom does that? It seems like she played the system in order to stay away. What makes me angry is realizing that if I hadn't pursued her, she would have gone to her grave without me ever seeing her, hugging her, holding her hand, stroking her hair, or telling her how much I loved her.

Rehashing these old feelings leads to anger against the one person I always seem to blame—myself.

KEVIN IJA BARNETT, SR.

I tell myself I should have researched more, searched earlier, dug deeper. Maybe I didn't seek hard enough to find my birth family. Maybe I should have started my quest earlier in life. I get upset at the many times I gave up on the search, surrendering to hopelessness. Had I pursued my biological family a little earlier, with more urgency, maybe I would have found them sooner.

Living with those failures—those maybes and shoulda-dones—that's the hard part.

How we act in the face of anger can define us. If we harbor hatred and anger it can derail our dreams, and sabotage our future.

Let's look at what anger feels like, how we can fight against and defeat it, and how we can transform what seems like a negative in our lives into a force for our own good, for success, for victory.

SHADOWS OF EMOTIONS

TOOLS FOR BATTLE

Think about this for a moment: When you experience anger, what does it feel like?

For me, anger makes me feel as if everything in my life has been hijacked. Stolen away. Anger rises when I feel robbed of control over my life.

Sometimes it comes out of a feeling of being sad and lonely. I wonder, What is my purpose on earth? Why was I chosen not to know my biological family?

That pain turns to helplessness. Then to hopelessness.

Then to anger.

I start crying. I grab a coat or something and squeeze it real tight. Sometimes I just sit in a chair and fold my arms over myself, and think about why I'm so angry. What good is it doing me? If I'm working out, I may hit the bag harder, putting all my hurt into each punch.

Controlling anger can be difficult. For some of us, it seems impossible. Anger makes us want to lash out, to hurt somebody, to make them feel the wounds we feel.

For me, the problems arise when I try to control my anger with sheer will.

Repressing anger might seem like a good idea. But it can be dangerous. By repressing it, there's no release valve for all that rage. By trying to hide it from others, we're hiding from our own feelings.

When we don't vent, we bottle up our rage. We bottle it up and bottle it up until it either eats us alive or explodes.

That conflict stirs up more and more rage. That unrelenting voice in your head won't allow it to stop until it's a rage-fueled firestorm burning out of control.

To gain control over anger, you need the tools to battle the feeling, then to release that emotion in a powerful, positive, constructive way.

SHADOWS OF EMOTIONS

What's your personal method for releasing anger? For finding the right balance for those feelings of rage? What do you do?

I work out. I hit the weights. I play video games. I concentrate on winning. After I'm finished, I tell myself I'm not going to be bothered anymore. My emotions are within my control. I engage in one of my Facebook groups, scrolling the stories of other adoptees like me.

We all need outlets. We all need safety valves. We need balance. Our emotions need control, and to control them our mindset needs a foundation of stability.

We need to teach ourselves and our family healthy coping skills for anger.

The truth is, I'm angrier now than I was at the start of my journey. It's not unusual to feel this. The further along the path one goes, the higher the mountains become, the deeper the valleys. Yet my anger doesn't wipe away all I've achieved—the relationships I've found, the siblings I've healed, the family I've reunited.

I'm thankful for the path I've walked, even with all the pain. When I look at other people's stories, I see what my story might have been—some still haven't found their siblings, or their parents. Or their parents refuse to talk to them, to acknowledge them. These folks are still locked in the dark about themselves. They're still a prisoner of their past.

I'm thankful my journey released me from that prison.

Being thankful is the antidote for anger. Being grateful for what we have, not what we lack. Even thankful for our failures, our frustration, which can be the vehicle for change, for transformation.

For healing.

Anger is a constant war, a daily battle. Being human, we all face anger. By dealing with our anger, by not hiding from our insecurities and trauma, by facing anger head-on instead of being bullied by it, the results can be life-changing.

Angry people become depressed people. And that's the subject for our next chapter.

CHAPTER FOUR

Depression

Depression is a deep, dark, twisted emotion. Many say depression feels like drowning. To me, depression feels like death.

According to estimates from the National Institute for Mental Health, nearly 10% of the American population will suffer at least one major episode of depression this year. It's most common in the 18-25 age group, and among those belonging to two or more ethnic races. Nearly half of those folks diagnosed with depression are also diagnosed with an anxiety disorder. And women are twice as likely to be affected with depression as men.

Depression hits folks like us—those seeking to find their birth families—harder than many of our friends and loved ones, I believe.

In our journey to find and connect with our family, the emotional ups-and-downs can be a rollercoaster, a wild and disorienting ride through grief, through peaks and valleys of feeling worthless, even unloved. And the emotional valleys in our hunt can feel deep, really deep.

Just think for a moment of the emotions and life events that can depress us.

Birthdays we missed. Bad news in our search. Dead ends without clues. Disappointment. Disillusionment. Guilt. Gloominess. Memories of old pain, physical torture, and abuse. Abandonment. Rejection. Dejection.

You name it. The list of emotions that can make us feel depressed isn't just deep and wide.

It's endless.

SHADOWS OF EMOTIONS

DEPRESSION BLUES

My story of depression is probably similar to yours.

Depression hits me hardest when family birthdays roll around. My brother's birthday, my grandfather's birthday, my grandmother's, my mother's—each time, I think about all the birthdays I've missed. All the family get-togethers I never shared.

According to my sister, my grandmother cooked gravy biscuits, which I never got to taste. I get depressed about that. I feel depressed that my brother died away from home, and I didn't get to visit him, that I missed his funeral.

Thoughts of missing all those family birthdays, those family moments and once-in-a-lifetime memories, can overwhelm me. I missed their birthdays, and they missed mine. Those moments will never come back again.

My father's birthday hits me especially hard. Each year when it comes up, just before

KEVIN IJA BARNETT, SR.

Memorial Day, I get monumentally depressed. In the last couple of years, I ventured up to his gravesite, just to talk to him, to tell my father some of the things I've accomplished. I even count to 10 in Japanese, because he was fluent in Japanese. That helps me connect with the man I never knew.

The fact that he died alone makes it even harder. I feel guilty about being "the only son," the one who wasn't there for him. I missed out on being able to tell him I loved him before he closed his eyes for the last time. Simple stuff like that really haunts me and affects me.

And Christmas? Don't even ask me about Christmas. When Christmastime rolls around I really get depressed, thinking back to being a small boy, and all the Christmases I missed with the blood relatives who've now passed away.

All the holidays are tough. But Christmas is the toughest.

SHADOWS OF EMOTIONS

Another source of depression is the relationship with my daughter—simply because I haven't had any type of relationship with her. We reconnected, around the time we took a DNA test together. Just before we received the results, she stopped talking to me. I didn't know why—but it's been months now since we've spoken. That depresses me—I wonder if my life would have turned out a little different for my daughter if I'd fostered that relationship earlier.

Sometimes it's those simple things that trigger depression. Things like just watching a TV show, that take my mind wandering back to all kind of what-ifs What-if I'd done this. What if I'd done that.

I think back to all the accomplishments and achievements my birth family missed out on—breaking my first board in martial arts, playing basketball in grammar school, ping-pong in Germany, becoming a champ at all kinds of things, then joining the military, going to war and coming back. Nobody from my blood family was there to cheer on those achievements, to give me a high-five, a congratulatory handshake or a hug.

The lack of human touch also affects me.

My mother doesn't embrace me as much as I thought she would. But that's okay; I understand. She doesn't talk to me on the phone unless I call. Again, I understand. The relationship between us isn't perfect, but it's what it is, and I'm undyingly grateful for it.

WARNING SIGNS

Unfortunately, there's a stigma of shame around depression.

We're not supposed to get depressed. We're not supposed to even talk about it. So it's hard to find help or to pinpoint the symptoms when they arise. But this is what experiencing depression feels like.

When we're depressed, we may experience anxiety, apathy, or a sense of hopelessness. Depressed people often isolate themselves, as they lose pleasure in activities they once enjoyed. It might be hard to concentrate on anything. Fatigue can set in. Weight gain—and even weight loss—can also be a warning sign, as is excessive crying or irritability. Sleep problems, and a preoccupation with death, can also make us act reckless like we've become a different person.

The way depression affects me is this:

When I'm depressed, I get in a slump, where I don't want to move. I'll stay in one spot, whether it's lying down or sitting up, and just stare at the ceiling. Stare and stare into outer space. My wife will see this, and come in to check on me, and soothe my heartache. "Are you all right?" She'll have to repeat that question two or three times before I hear it, and finally answer, "Yes."

"What are you thinking about?" she'll ask.

I'll answer, "Nothing," because I really don't want her worrying about me. Then I'll go back to staring. Staring and staring, in deep meditation, unable to stop my mind from wandering and thinking, until I finally break out of it.

How I snap out of a depressive episode is always different.

I'll play video games, to release the tension, to free my mind. Sometimes I'll call up a friend or a relative. I'll think about the family relationships I've healed, all those I've connected with, and that will snap me out of it, and ease my frustration.

In the past few years, I've organized a family barbecue cookout. My father's side of the family, my mother's side, my wife's side, and my adoptive family have all come—60 to 75 people, from all over Connecticut, Florida, Pennsylvania, Maryland, Delaware, New Jersey, and Washington State. We get together and I open my house up to everybody, so we can meet and eat and talk.

SHADOWS OF EMOTIONS

Originally, one of my cousins had hosted the reunion barbecue. Unfortunately, he passed away. Right before however, we talked. He told me, "Cousin, you know you've got to do this next year." When he passed away, I made a promise to myself to carry on the tradition that my cousin put his heart and soul into.

Another form of therapy is connecting with my Facebook group—those folks like myself, who are searching for their blood kin. I'll hear stories similar to mine—somebody posting Today is my mother's birthday, and I feel blue, or posting something like, Why do I have all these feelings for the family I've never known? It's hard to process all the emotions that can hit us, that can trouble us, and sharing my feelings on Facebook makes me feel like what I'm experiencing is common, that I'm not a stranger, that in fact, I don't have it that bad.

That brings a calmness, a peace over me.

The truth is, my struggle is probably similar to yours. When I get trapped in depression, I'll do anything to stop dwelling on my problem, to switch up my mindset, to get out of my hopelessness before it turns into anger. Those emotions can weave together, and depression can turn to anger, and anger can trigger a violent outburst that quickly flames out of control.

Climbing out of depression is a daily process. It's one moment at a time. One step at a time. Step by step.

Just remember: You are not alone.

Other folks just like you are walking the same walk, feeling what you feel. Reach out to them, for comfort, or when you're feeling the first signs of depression. Find a professional counselor in your area. Reaching out for help, and then helping others when they need it, is the first step to healing those old emotional scars.

Fortunately, it's not all sorrow and pain on this journey. There are powerful, positive emotions too, as you'll see in our next chapter.

CHAPTER FIVE

Joy

Let's switch gears.

Let's change the subject.

Let's reset the mood, from darkness to light.

Instead of talking about all the sad, depressing emotions we experience in life, all the trials and tribulations, all the trauma and drama each of us faces, let's begin to discuss some of the positive emotions life blesses us with.

Let's talk about joy.

No matter how great your struggle has been, no matter how many battles you might have fought and lost, I bet each of you has experienced moments of joy on this journey.

Joy is the counterbalance. The balance to all the sorrow and sadness.

Joy is the foundation for our inner strength. Joy gives us courage, to march forward, to take leaps of faith. Seeking joy motivates us to rise when we fall, to stand when we want to crawl, to overcome our problems.

Even in our darkest times, our most depressed state of mind, moments of joy can be found—if we just look for them. If we are open to them.

Prior to writing my first book, *Living My Shadows: Dreams Do Come True*, there were many incredible moments along the path that gave me joy, even when things looked bleak.

I remember my phone call to social services, to the state of New Jersey, seeking answers to the questions about my ancestry. I'd told them the information I'd previously received, that my grandmother had passed away at a certain time in Virginia, details that I'd never had any luck in following up, that had led me to nothing but dead ends.

And I recall the young lady from social services listening intently to my story, then suddenly telling me, "Wait a minute. Your grandmother did pass away, but it wasn't in Virginia."

"It wasn't?" I said, shocked.

"No," the young lady replied. "It was Asbury Park, in 1979."

Her words sent a shiver through me. Her words stunned me. And as soon as I hung up the phone, and the reality of what she'd said hit me, I felt my heart pounding. I felt electrified with this feeling of joy.

That was my first glimmer of hope. Now I was off and running on my search. For years I'd been chasing a rabbit down a rabbit hole—now all of a sudden I'd been handed this new information. Now I could actually continue my search, with hope.

All my years of hopelessness faded. My search for blood kin suddenly had a purpose, a reason to keep hunting, pursuing.

And inspired by this piece of information, my entire life felt wrapped in this warm blanket of joy. Joy for the very first time on my long and twisting journey.

Pure joy. Elation. Excitement.

Now I had a year (1979) and a place (Asbury Park). Prior to that, my search had begun to seem hopeless. Even worse than hopeless—it seemed pointless. All that searching, searching, searching, leading to dead ends. What was I wasting my time?

Now things were getting closer to finding the truth.

Soon afterward, I began connecting with blood relatives. I learned about a family connection to the Bahamas. I tracked down some blood cousins through DNA, through Ancestry.com. I met one of them in person when they came to our family reunion. I FaceTimed another.

That was the turning point. For the first time, I began experiencing more and more joy on my search.

It wouldn't be the last time, however.

Feeling that joy, that elation gave me a sense of relief. I became intensely emotional. I cried when I learned the information about my grandmother. Suddenly there was a possibility I might meet my birth mother—I knew she was alive now. I had hope that my dreams would come true.

That hope came directly from those incredible moments of optimism, of possibility.

That hope came from joy.

FINDING FEAR IN JOY

In the middle of all this joy however, the strangest emotion also hit me.

I felt fear.

KEVIN IJA BARNETT, SR.

I felt scared.

What am I so scared of? I wondered.

First of all, even though I was a step closer to locating my family, I was scared I would be rejected by them. Sure, I might locate them, I might track them down, I might know their names and where they lived, but they still may end up rejecting me, after all these years.

So that was the scary part. Even in my joy, there were times I was filled with anxiety. I worried things wouldn't turn out well. I worried the situation would lead to another dead end. I worried I'd be abandoned again—this time by the family I'd spent decades tracking down.

I feared I'd lose everything I'd worked so hard to bring to life. It had happened to others. All I could do was hope and pray that wouldn't happen to me.

Even in the depths of my greatest fears, however, I knew I could turn to my Facebook group for support. I'd seen messages from others who'd experienced the same thing, a feeling of joy on the journey, only to see it evaporate into feelings of fear, of rejection, of hopelessness.

That was the process. Find the balance. Stay rooted in hope and joy. Fight my fears. And continue the struggle.

Yet my heart battled those fears constantly. Thank God I'd experienced those moments of joy! Once I'd found joy, I could always tap into it, to overpower the hopelessness, the possibility of disappointment, of failure. I could take a leap of faith. I could take the chance of being rejected, and hope for a favorable outcome.

All because I'd experienced joy.

I learned to feed off this joy. And I kept feeding off it. Feeling that joy again became my motive, my inspiration. It became the driving factor that kept me going, no matter how many times life hurled me into the ditch, no matter how rocky the road became.

Soon I began finding names of my blood kin. I found Cora Hodge, my grandmother's name. That led me to Thomas Hodge. Then I learned my mother's name was Lois. Suddenly I could see how these names were associated with me. Each time I received new information—whether it was from the state, or somebody in my Facebook group—each time it happened, I found myself crying tears of joy

Now I had a sense of belonging. A sense of connection. Of knowing who I am, where I come from. That belonging-feeling gave me joy—intense, overwhelming joy.

A JOY LIKE NO OTHER

Since writing my first book, that same joyous feeling has returned time and time again on my search.

Meeting my mom, of course, was a moment of joy I'll never forget. I met face-to-face with my mom, my brother, and my sister. That was a moment of amazing jubilation, of

SHADOWS OF EMOTIONS

celebration—here I was, standing in a soul food restaurant in Asbury Park, holding my mom, embracing her, and she was reaching out and touching my hand for the first time! Wow! I could look straight into the eyes of the lady who'd given me birth.

Suddenly all my negative thoughts and fears vanished. I was happy, so happy that I couldn't even cry. For 56 years, I'd wondered who I looked like, who I received the color of my skin from, the color of my eyes, the shape of my head.

That was the first time everything came together.

Nothing compares to that moment, to that level of joy. It was joyous to see this roomful of people, all of whom looked like me.

I'd found my kinfolk. My flesh and blood. My bloodline.

I felt connected. I belonged here.

That, to me, was a joy like no other.

KEVIN IJA BARNETT, SR.

The next greatest joy I felt was learning who my father was. Now I had the two central connections, the two deepest links, my ancestral foundation—my mother and father.

Soon I started meeting family members—on my mother's side, on my father's side. I found a cousin who lived a few miles from me. Another cousin I met soon passed away, so I was grateful for the time I had with her. We held a reunion for my father's side of the family, in Texas. I met my father's only living sibling, at her 100th birthday party.

At these first meetings, I was finally able to talk with family members, tell them who I was. At first, I was apprehensive because no one knew me. But my cousin—who I'd spoken with over the phone from New York—said, "Just be patient. When you get the chance to tell your story, they are going to gravitate to you. That's how Southern people are." It was so good! My cousin made me a quilt of my favorite college football team, the Florida Gators—she comes

SHADOWS OF EMOTIONS

from a long line of Gator fans. At that moment, I felt embraced by everyone in the family.

Another joyful occasion occurred the day one of my sons met my mother. My second oldest son was intensely touched—for the first time, he'd come into contact with someone who looked like him, other than his dad. He was amazed by that. So this was a joyous moment of family connection.

Perhaps the most overpowering moment in the last two years was my first family birthday party, with my mother actually singing "Happy birthday" to me. My first Mother's Day was also very significant. That day, I experienced the whole range of emotions: joy, sadness, tears, and happiness all at once. The fact that my mom sang happy birthday to me for the very first time in 56 years is a memory I'll replay in my mind forever.

All these memories are powerful—and they all return to that first joyful phone call with the social services lady in New Jersey. Joy is the thing that gave me hope and that kept me going for a long time. All these moments and memories of joy are so much more powerful than all the negative feelings I'd experienced. Once I felt joy, it gave me the strength to continue moving forward and to accomplish what my heart had always yearned for.

Truly that joy is beyond anything I can even put into words.

I thank God I'm so blessed to have lived this long, to have survived through the hopeless times, to have struggled and overcome and been given the chance to experience these moments.

JOY FUELS THE JOURNEY

Did these moments match what I'd always hoped? What I dreamed of, all these years?

Truth is, they were so much more than I could ever hope for. To feel accepted,

SHADOWS OF EMOTIONS

connected, to belong, to no longer have to hide in the shadows changed everything.

And I am still finding family members now. I've tracked down over 300 family members. I've contacted some over the phone. Some I've met in person, and some over social media. I've talked to people from my father's homeland, in the Bahamas and the West Indies.

I started a site on Facebook called " I Am Hodge" for the family to connect. It started off with just two people—now there are over 250. Just thinking about that overwhelms me.

The whole journey can be overwhelming. Yet the journey is the thing that's gotten me through life. Because I have these feelings—joyful feelings, and sad feelings too—I feel motivated to continue the search and to accomplish even more.

These moments I've shared are the main events I've experienced joy and happiness from, on this incredible journey. These experiences molded me for the rest of my life, filling me with a spark when I felt tapped out, motivating me anytime things went south, when the struggle felt overpowering when my dream felt unachievable. Ignited and sparked by these moments of joy and happiness is what gave me hope.

There is so much power in having hope.

Hope is the spark. Hope is the fuel that fires us up, that drives us to march forward, to step out of the shadows. We'll dig deeper into this emotion called hope, in my next chapter.

CHAPTER SIX

Hope

In our previous chapter, we left behind the negative emotions and talked about joy. Let's keep moving forward in our discussion, and talk about another positive emotion—an emotion every human being on the planet feels—an emotion that kept coming up again and again in our chapter on joy.

That emotion is hope.

Everybody on earth hopes. From the youngest child to the eldest on the planet, everybody wishes. Everybody desires and dreams and yearns.

Each of us carries our own personal hopes. We hope for a happier life. We hope of a better job, a higher income, a bigger house, a healthier lifestyle. We experience hope for ourselves and hope for others.

When we think about the word hope, the emotion we feel is always positive, always optimistic, always encouraging.

Usually, hope is based on a person being caught in a situation or a place or a relationship they want out of—sometimes desperately want out of—and they're hoping and praying for something better to come along. Something that will change or transform their lives. Something that will rescue them, something that will save the day. They are waiting for a life-changing event with great expectation, with conviction, with optimism. They are holding onto a promise that things are going to get better.

On my own personal journey, in the years before I wrote my first book, I was living on hope, on dreams, on prayers, on promises. I was being driven by the hope of one day meeting my original bloodline, my birth family, of what that day would be like.

Hope is what kept me alive.

Hope is how I made it through each day.

Hope was my greatest driving force, the inner motivation that drove me to continue the journey, no matter how despairing I often felt, no matter how many obstacles or pitfalls I faced.

Ever since the dark days of being a foster child, I'd held onto one specific hope: The hope that one day I'd finally meet my blood family, my mom and dad, my siblings, my grandparents.

As a child, I hoped that my blood family was living a better life than I was. I hoped they were happy. Additionally, I held hopes and dreams about what my father looked like. Was he a tall guy? A small guy? A heavy guy, a skinny guy? And what did my mother look like? Was there a part of me that looked like her, that spoke like her, that thought like her? I also hoped I had a twin, a brother, somebody who dressed like me, who had the same mannerisms as me, somebody I could share my inner thoughts and childhood desires with. I craved that bond, that super-connection, that brotherhood nobody else on the face of the earth but a brother could understand.

As a youngster, I wondered what part of Africa my family had come from—at the time, I believed everybody just went straight from Africa to the United States. I knew that when I finally met up with my family, it would satisfy all my curiosities, and answer all these questions. It would be a positive feeling unlike any I'd ever experienced.

In my mind, I created a mental picture of what this meeting would look like. At night I'd hold that vision in my brain, letting it spark and energize me during the lonely daytime hours in my foster home.

Years later, I'd find out that my brother did, in fact, look a lot like me. He was born two years prior to my birth, though he passed away before I found my family. The strange thing is that we also shared a lot of the same habits, the same mannerisms. Our personalities were similar. So the brotherhood, the connection, the bond I'd dreamed of, yearned for, hoped for, came true.

DEEPER HOPES

My hopes for my mother and father ran even deeper.

I hoped my mom would accept me, for who I really am. Knowing she'd given me up, abandoned me, left me for foster care at birth, triggered negative emotions and self-doubts for most of my adult life. My hope was that upon finally meeting me she'd never again disown me. I hoped she'd have a different view of me, as a grown man. I hoped she knew that no matter what else, I wouldn't blame or disappoint my mother. She'd tried to hide from me, the first few times I contacted her. Though this frustrated me greatly, I understood, and never blamed her.

KEVIN IJA BARNETT, SR.

I still had no information on my father. Thus I was hoping my mother could share some information. Where was he from? How did they meet? Did they discuss giving me up at birth together? What exactly was his role in the whole thing?

To this day, I'm not 100% certain my father knew anything about me, or if he found out about me later. I remained hopeful I'd one day learn the truth.

I never pursued most of these family secrets with my mother. She was getting up in age, falling in and out of dementia. Some days, it was impossible to get anything out of her. From speaking with her sister and with the state of New Jersey, I learned she had two other children at the time, and couldn't bear the thought of taking care of a third. That's how I wound up in the foster care system.

But all that's in the past now. In the year and a half since writing my first book, my hopes for deeper family bonds have grown abundant.

SHADOWS OF EMOTIONS

I still hope and pray to find more family members. I continue to get closer to my brother and sister. Knowing I can't make up for the lost time is hard—at times, we still feel like strangers—so I try my best to enjoy the moments I have with them now, praying over time that we can become closer. As the days and months pass, that connection gets stronger and stronger.

Even with tighter family connections, I still feel some of the old negative emotions—anger, frustration, sadness. I keep these emotions to myself. I don't want my family to see me harboring any old pain or regret—just knowing my bloodline is alive helps me overcome any bitterness at feeling cheated, ungrateful, or robbed of my dreams by my past.

Gratitude for what I have now is a powerful weapon, along with hope. I know there are many other adoptees in much worse situations than I am. I remain grateful for what I have and blessed if someday I have even more.

HOPE CHANGES

Thirty years ago, before I was reunited with my family, my hopes looked and felt much different. The dynamics have changed now.

For one thing, I don't need to hope to one day find out who I look like. The hopes that fill my heart now are more about discovering my family history–tracking down and learning more about my relatives, my kinfolk, and bringing my relatives together. Currently, we're scattered all over the map. Some of us live right around the corner from each other, and some live in a far corner of the globe.

The hope is I can be that beam of light in the family. To inspire my bloodline through my own story, my own journey.

As my story changes, my hopes change too.

My story's not just about me anymore; it's about what I can do for others. It's about helping others seek their own answers. It's about giving a face to the faceless, and hope to the hopeless.

A lot of my own hope comes from the Facebook groups I'm involved with.

The fact that other adoptees are going through many of the same things I've experienced has blessed me with a different perspective. Reading the stories on the Facebook site, I appreciate all I have, and all I'm still yearning to find, knowing that others in my same situation may never find their mother and father, may never have a relationship with their birth family.

Many will never experience the joy I've had, nor the moments I've shared with my blood family. That's a shame. For me, this journey has been like a holy quest. It's provided me a purpose for living when I felt life held no purpose. It's provided me answers to the most profound questions a man can ask.

People used to ask me, "Where do you come from? Who do you look like?" It used to be that I couldn't answer those questions because I truly didn't know.

Finding those answers was the answer to my hope. When I needed hope, my Facebook group was always there, as one of my greatest supporters. My support network was always there to lend hope to me, even when things looked bleak.

Somebody in the group would post something encouraging, and lift my spirits. Somebody else would see I was downhearted, and email me and say, "Be encouraged. Don't give up. You'll find them. Just be ready." They always reminded me to stay ready, because the search can always go either way.

Sometimes it would just be somebody posting an update: They met their folks, they found a sibling, they received a hopeful result from their inquiries. Every posting I read was a blessing, a spark of motivation, a ray of hope. To this day, I still visit the site often. I congratulate those who have tracked down their parents or met their family, and I express my sorrow and my remorse to those who share a negative experience, whose first meeting with their brother or sister went awry, who continue to be turned away by their bloodline.

The support we share for each other never stops. We lean on each other. We share our good days and our bad days. We have a lifelong bond. We have common fears and common dreams. We all remain hopeful.

Of course, there were others outside of my Facebook group who blessed me with hope and encouraged me during my journey.

My wife, my sons and my grandmother (who passed away back in the 1990s) were my most ardent and my closest supporters. My grandmother was the one who'd actually met my father; she always told me: "Don't worry. Just have faith. You've got to have faith. If finding your family was meant to happen, it'll happen."

KEVIN IJA BARNETT, SR.

SWIMMING IN HOPE

When I think about the word hope, and what hope looks like, what it feels like, it's incredibly difficult to put into words.

What does the emotion of hope feel like?

Speaking personally, hope feels like the action of swimming. It's like you're swimming from one side of the pool to the other side underwater, praying you can hold your breath the whole way. I used to do this at my local YMCA: I'd jump into the deep end of their Olympic-sized pool, and dive underwater, swimming and holding my breath for as long as I could. Sometimes I needed to come up for air, but I'd go back underwater again, until I finally made it to the other side, safe and sound.

That's hope. That's what hope feels like.

Hope is like there's always something to strive for. Our striving never ends. Even though you might reach your goal, you make another

SHADOWS OF EMOTIONS

goal, and you keep going. Each time, you hope to reach the next step, the finish line. You hope to do better today than yesterday.

Hope is a feeling of encouragement within oneself. Hope pushes us to keep driving forward, moving onward toward the next step, the next goal, the next achievement. To achieve anything in life, you must have hope.

Hope is an intangible. You can't see it. You can't touch it. Yet you know it's there.

To stop hoping is to lose faith in something bigger than yourself. If you didn't think you could make it to the other side of the swimming pool, you'd stop. You'd give up. There would be no reason to keep going. What keeps you going is that hope that you'll reach the end of the pool, that you'll come up out of the water on the other side. That you'll be able to breathe again.

You'd quit, without hope. You'd turn around, and go back where you started.

You'd drown.

You'd die.

Without hope.

But with hope, with prayers, with dreams and inspiration, we keep moving right along. We keep battling our doubts and uncertainties. We trust that someday our trials will end, our family will be reunited, and our hopes will be answered.

Hope is a powerful weapon. It's the mighty sword we carry each day in our fight against one of the darkest shadows of emotions each one of us faces.

That shadow is called rejection.

CHAPTER SEVEN

Rejection

In my first book, *Living My Shadows*, I spoke a lot about the emotional shadow called rejection.

Without a doubt, rejection is the most painful emotion of all for an adoptee or a foster child to speak about. Even in the best of times, it's an emotion our minds battle to hide from, and one we struggle to overcome every single day, in every circumstance, in every situation.

Living with rejection breeds fear.

Being abandoned breeds mistrust.

Feeling disowned and disconnected breeds emotional turmoil.

Rejection can also breed anger, anxiety, and depression. In some folks, it can even lead to self-destruction or outbursts of violence.

Rejection was one of the most difficult things I had to deal with, coming out of the foster care system. Being rejected by my birth mother made me feel abandoned by everybody as if I'd been dumped in a ditch and left to fend for myself when it came to everything—food, shelter, protection, comfort.

Looking around my life, I'd see rejection everywhere. As a teenager or a young adult, trying to date a girl or form a relationship I struggled with anxiety about being rejected. Seeing a girl who was attracted to me, sometimes I'd choose not to speak to them because my confidence level was low, and I was afraid of rejection. Even as an adult, as a married man who'd accomplished many near-impossible things, I feared rejection because my mother had rejected me at birth.

I struggled to establish friendships. I struggled to create bonds. I was wary of establishing close relationships.

All these roads lead back to that original rejection by my birth mom.

Rejection can destroy you.

Or it can make you stronger.

REJECTION AT MY DOORSTEP

When I called my birth family for the first time, rejection was right there, waiting at the doorstep.

My birth sister answered the phone. She didn't know who was calling; I knew I'd gotten the contact information correct and I'd called the right number. In my heart, I knew this woman on the other end of the line was my sister. Yet hearing me announce to her who I was she hesitated, then said to me, "Listen, I have to go," and hung up the phone.

Right there, rejection almost defeated me. Rejection nearly won the day. I needed to regroup—because of all the rejection I'd faced already, I didn't know if I'd have the courage or the inner strength to do this again.

"You know what?" I finally told myself. "I'm not giving up. I need to try this, one more time."

That second time, I was successful. I'd broken through.

The first time I met my biological brother, I thought for sure I was going to be rejected. Yet everybody seemed cool. No rejection at all. Except that now, I started worrying about how I'd be accepted by the whole extended family. I struggled with rejection anxiety about the way they'd perceive me.

Rejection was always at the forefront of my emotions. It felt like I was in a race, where everybody was a mile and a half ahead of me, and I was always playing catch-up. Being successful in tracking down my family didn't suppress or subdue my fear of rejection. That fear remained there—it'll probably be there, until the day I die.

Learning how to deal with it would become my life's journey.

LIVING IN REJECTION MODE

Fear of rejection is always bubbling in my head. No matter if I'm hanging out with friends, or at the grocery store, or on the phone with my children.

Rejection issues surface every day.

When I'm texting people, sometimes I don't receive a text message in reply. We've all been there, right? But in my head, that message I didn't receive is a form of rejection—it's not intentional, but it's a feeling of being neglected and cast-off that I have to deal with.

I've learned not to always look at things in rejection mode. Sometimes it's just the way life is. But because rejection was there at the very start of my journey, at the beginning of my life, it feels like I am always facing rejection in one way or another.

I've had to live my life learning to face and overcome rejection because that's where my story started. Rejection made me who I am today.

Yet it's not all negative—there are many positive things to learn out of being rejected.

When we're rejected, we can use that as motivation, and say to ourselves, "Well, I will just prove these people wrong. I'll prove myself to them." It gives us that extra rush, that boost of "I'll prove them wrong" determination and willpower.

Then sometimes you learn you can't prove other people wrong, which proves to yourself that you don't always have to prove anything, that sometimes there's really nothing to prove. Life is more about enjoying the moment than it is trying to rewrite the past.

The past is the past. Rewriting it is impossible. Replaying it doesn't change anything. Though worrying about rejection will always be there, bubbling around in my head, letting go of that fear and moving past it is where I found my greatest healing.

REJECTION PAYBACK

Does the rejection I faced and felt as a child feel any different, now that I'm an adult?

Truth is, it doesn't. That pain and hurt of rejection are always going to feel the same, no matter how my status changes, no matter how much older and wiser I become.

That painful feeling I had when I was born and left at some stranger's doorstep will never leave—I can compartmentalize it, and blot it out of my mind temporarily, but it will always be there.

Sometimes I close my eyes at night, and think back to when I was four or five years old, lying in my bed in a foster home and wondering, Who is my mother? Where is she? I recall being sixteen or seventeen and asking myself that same question. It's still hard for me to comprehend or fathom the idea of my mother bringing me into this world, looking at her newborn baby in the eyes, and then handing me off to somebody else.

It's a surreal feeling. Hard as I try to understand, to connect the dots, they remain disconnected.

I just hope and pray my own daughter doesn't feel that way, that she didn't spend her life wondering, Who is my father? I suppose she may carry these same feelings—after all, she was rejected by me. Though it was unintentional, I still was not there in her life and missed the first 30 years of her upbringing.

Is the rejection I feel from my daughter some form of payback? I may never know for certain. Having to face and overcome rejection my entire life, I've taken great pains to make sure other people—especially my own family—never feel rejected.

But our families aren't the only place we see rejection. We see rejection everywhere. Whether it's people from other countries trying to enter the United States to find a better life, or individuals in our society who are rejected because of the way they look, the way they think, the way they dress or talk, rejection is real, and it's an unpleasant fact of life.

Rejection is a world-wide human theme. We all have similar rejection stories. Although I feel very cognizant of being abandoned when I was a child, and still have trouble shaking those feelings, deep down I know I'm not the only one.

I'm not alone. You have rejection stories, too.

REJECTION STRATEGIES

How does one heal the hurt of rejection?

Simple: Communicating our feelings with those we love.

Talking about rejection, sharing our feelings with our family, and communicating our need to overcome that old trauma is the first step.

One of my sisters and I have talked a lot about rejection. She feels the pain I've been through—that pain affected her too because she was robbed of having an older brother all these years. She was robbed of experiencing the everyday things brothers and sisters experience. My sister still feels robbed, and we've had deep discussions about that. Hearing that her perspective is both similar to mine, and how it's different, has illuminated and inspired me.

Since reuniting, my sister and I have shared many emotions, good and bad. We've also discussed how I feel toward my mother. At times, I feel guilty that I'm the one who's abandoned her—at other times, that old Why? question keeps coming up, haunting me. Why did she abandon me? It's hard to shake not knowing the answer. It's hard not knowing if I'll ever be as close to my mother as I'd dreamed I might be.

These unanswered questions and emotions are things I deal with, every single day. When the feelings become too painful, too stressful, powerful, I find myself putting up a wall—a rejection wall. That way, nobody can reach me or hurt me.

Expressing myself to my family has helped bring those walls down. The walls are coming down slowly. They may never come down completely, but just watching them crumble is a healthy thing.

Speaking about my situation publicly has also helped tear down the walls. When I share my personal story at speaking engagements, rejection is one of my main themes. Telling folks how I've grown from a foster child to being reunited with my biological family, I see the light of motivation to take that same journey shining in their eyes. It's never easy talking about rejection—sometimes when I speak about being given up for adoption at birth, I tear up. The past I've lived through is still painful and remains a touchy subject.

Hearing what others in the same situation have been through, and how they've overcome that situation, can heal us. That's the motivation for me telling my story.

So take a moment, and think about your story.

Think about the rejection you've faced. Think about the pain you've lived through.

Then I think about what a victory over that painful rejection would look like. Think about what overcoming that old trauma would feel like.

There's a path for each of us to battle and defeat those old rejection feelings.

It's called moving on.

We can't remain stuck in the past if we hope for a future that includes being reunited with our family. Changing the way, we perceive the past is one healing adjustment each of us can make. Just because we received abandonment in the past doesn't mean we're doomed to receive it again and again.

Move on.

If you have a hurdle, an obstacle, a mountain you need to get past, find a way to go around it. Take another direction. Find another road. Blaze your own path, if you need to.

Move on.

Remaining stuck in the same old spot, the same hopeless situation makes us prone to depression, anger, even suicidal thoughts.

We can't remain mad at the world because we feel stuck in our situation. We can take action.

Move on.

Rejection feelings are painful, but they can be defeated. As I said before, each one of us can use rejection to either destroy us or to make us stronger.

It's your choice.

Making that choice and moving forward will fill us with peace—and that emotion is the subject of my next chapter.

CHAPTER EIGHT

Peace

Writing about the emotion of peace has been the most difficult topic of all in this book. It's been a battle, a challenge, a monumental struggle. Tackling the subject of peace has taken me to the darkest recesses and the deepest depths of my soul.

Why?

Because two days ago, my mom—my birth mother, the woman I spent the first 59 years of my life trying to find, trying to forgive, trying to reconcile and reunite with—passed away.

And as I write these words, I am bombarded by every emotion imaginable. I am trying to hang in there. I am struggling to find the right words.

I am trying to find peace.

LOSING FAMILY, FINDING PEACE

It's difficult to put into words what I am feeling now, knowing my mom is gone. All kinds of crazy feelings have been running through my heart and my mind. Hurt. Sadness. Gratitude. Pain. Happy memories, too. Everything is mixed up. I cry frequently.

Last night, I felt my mom was here with me, talking to me, telling me she loved me, that she did the best she could for me. I kept hearing her voice, feeling her presence.

Yet though my heart is broken, my heart keeps returning to a feeling of peace. And my mind keeps repeating over and over the idea of peace. Though I didn't have time to prepare for her death, and though tears and sadness seem to appear at a moment's notice, I am finding peace in the middle of all these emotions.

SHADOWS OF EMOTIONS

There is peace in knowing that, at long last, I'd been reunited with my mom. I found her. After 59 years, we were reunited.

Together, we came to a place of peace in our relationship. Though we struggled at times, both of us found a place where we could let go of the past and be grateful for what we had now.

One of the last things my mother said to me was that she tried to do all she could to love me and that she hoped I wouldn't blame her for the pain I experienced as a child, in foster care.

"Please forgive me," she said, as she was dying.

Those three words healed me. I told her I'd forgiven her a long time ago, that she no longer needed to worry about my forgiveness. Those words helped her make peace with herself, and with all the painful situations she imagined I'd faced.

I wanted her to have no regrets. No shame. No guilt.

KEVIN IJA BARNETT, SR.

I wanted her to have peace.

At the end, I was able to whisper in her ear that I loved her. She replied that she loved me too, and I left her with those last words pounding in my heart. Soon thereafter, the phone rang, and the family called to tell us she was gone.

In that moment of her passing, I felt a strange tranquility, a serenity, a calm, a peace. It was the peace of knowing we'd done all we could to heal our relationship. It was a sense of peace within myself, the peace of this chapter in my life ending, of closure. Though there remained questions that would never be asked and questions that would never be answered, those questions no longer mattered. The fact that my mom loved me, that she'd accepted me, that I accepted she'd done what she had to do, and what she believed was best for me—giving me a life she couldn't provide at the time—that knowledge healed me.

SHADOWS OF EMOTIONS

At that moment, all the old hurt went away. All the old pain vanished.

All the years I thought my mom just didn't love me any longer mattered. She'd done what she felt was best, as my mother. She carried the pain of abandoning me in her heart for nearly 60 years. How could I not see her sacrifice and the love in that?

I was suddenly able to see the love I'd brought to her life, too. My sister comforted me with stories about the joy I'd brought my mom. She no longer had to hide from the past. Facing our past, she became more relaxed, laughing and joking. Those three years we had together provided her with a kind of joy she'd been missing.

Hearing those stories gave me additional closure. They reminded me of the many happy memories those three years had blessed me with.

In just three years, I accomplished everything I'd set out to achieve. In three years,

I achieved milestone after milestone. First of all, I found my birth mom. She celebrated my birthday and sang "Happy Birthday" to me. I celebrated Mother's Day with her and bought her flowers, every Mother's Day since. I invited her over to my house, introduced her to my kids and some of my grandkids. She was able to hear about my accomplishments and tell me she was proud of me.

Most importantly, I was able to touch and hold my mom for the very first time and look into her eyes and tell her I loved her.

That was amazing. And it was a moment more powerful than I'd ever dreamed or imagined.

Sometimes I wonder if she stayed alive so long to make sure she had the time to make peace with me. Any time I wasn't around, she'd ask my siblings, "Where's Kevin? I haven't seen him in a while." If I didn't visit for a week, she'd question my family. "Hey, listen, where's Kevin at?"

I can't ask for more than that.

THE GREATEST PEACE OF ALL

It's amazing that my mom's passing brought peace to all the turmoil I'd felt in my life. For more than 50 years, I'd been wanting and waiting for that moment of being reunited.

The very first time I heard her voice on the phone, I knew it was my mom. For perhaps the first time in my journey, I experienced peace. No longer did I feel my life was ruled by turbulence.

I just wanted to remain in that moment. It's what I had always been seeking. That feeling of calm. Of closure. Of connection. Of finding peace, within myself.

That moment changed who I am. Suddenly I knew where I'd come from, and I could trust where I was going. It was like the first day of being born. Now I had the bond only a mother and son could share.

At that moment, I no longer felt robbed. I no longer felt cheated. I felt prepared for my next journey.

I appreciate those three years we had, because of the journey I'd been on to reach my goal. My journey gave me a whole new perspective on life, and on death. What felt like a curse in the past I now realized was my greatest blessing.

My mom's passing was the culmination of my lifelong journey to find peace. Knowing I'll never see my mom again is hard. It's real hard. But she prepared me for it.

Peace didn't come the way I thought it would. As I said at the start, this was the hardest chapter to write, the most difficult emotion to explore. The struggle to find peace in the middle of my greatest loss made me ask the tough questions. How could I find my birth mom, then so quickly lose her? Yet I found that peace—the greatest peace of all—in our story of reconciliation, forgiveness, and love.

CHAPTER NINE

The "Why?" Questions

Since the passing of my birth mom, I've been struggling with a headful of the same old questions running through my mind.

The vast majority of these questions revolve around the word Why?

Why me? Why now? Why my mom? Why didn't I find her earlier in my life? Why couldn't I have reunited with my mom when she was younger, when I was a child when we would have had so many years together ahead of us?

I spoke about "the rollercoaster of emotions" previously in this book. I've been riding that dizzying emotional rollercoaster now for the past week. Up and down. Up and down. Then up and down again.

To help me deal with these cascading emotions, these overwhelming feelings, I thought it best to confront the feelings head-on, and talk for a chapter about all the "Why?" questions that adoptees and those struggling to find their biological families battle against.

THE HOLE THAT NEEDS FILLING

For years, my mind wandered with thoughts about the family members I'd never met, and the biological bloodline I feared I might never find. Deep down, I knew my birth mother and father were out there, somewhere. Yet for years before I found them, during the decades I was still desperately hunting and searching, what consumed my thoughts over and over weren't my dreams about what the day we reunited might look like. It wasn't hope for the future, or regret about the past.

SHADOWS OF EMOTIONS

It was those never-ending, non-stop "Why?" questions.

Why exactly did my mother give me up at birth? Was it because of my father? Was it because I was ugly or deformed? No matter how hard I tried to empathize with my mom, and whatever situation she'd felt herself trapped in, I just couldn't wrap my mind around a mother giving her child up. I didn't know if I was an only child at the time, or if she already had other children. Was that it? Were there just too many mouths to feed, too many children for a single mom to handle?

Why did she allow me to live, yet not want to be a part of my life?

The "Why?" questions continued to pound my brain.

In desperation, I even asked God "Why?", trying to understand. Why me, God? Why did you let this happen? If you're the God of compassion and love, why allow me to be abandoned? Why allow me to almost die? Why allow me to suffer all these years? Why did you let me be adopted by the Crawfords, and placed into the foster care system, where I was abused and tortured? Why did I need to be obsessed with finding my family, instead of accepting the loving family that adopted me as all I really needed? And why, God, couldn't you have taken somebody else, instead of my mom?

The emotions I experienced from those unanswered questions ran the gamut, from anger to depression to sorrow, from hope and joy to hopelessness and remorse.

I suddenly realized that things hadn't changed much, as far as my emotions, just because I'd finally tracked down my birth family.

The old "Why?" questions still popped up. And now, there were new questions.

While I understood the reasons behind my mother giving me up, I suddenly struggled with questions about our new relationship. Why do I sometimes feel like a stranger, in her presence? I wondered. Why, after 50 years of searching, do I still have these deep feelings of anger? Why do I still have this emptiness inside, of not truly knowing who I am? Why didn't I find my birth father in time, before he died, so I could meet him and touch him and hug him and shake his hand?

As an adult, the "Why?" questions had changed from those of my childhood. Yet the emotions ran just as deep—in some cases, deeper and heavier.

They felt heavier because for years I'd hoped to know all the answers. Now, I struggled to realize that some of my questions would never be answered. That put a tremendous weight on my heart, heavier than the weight of my childhood.

Sure, the answers I'd found gave me peace. The answers gave me satisfaction and closure. And they filled me with a sense of completeness, and connection. Even though I would never meet many of my bloodline, I knew now who they were, what they looked like, and some of the histories of their lives.

That knowledge made me feel whole. It gave me a connection. It gave me a bond with my mother and father, my brothers and sisters.

Yet it didn't fill the hole of wanting the one thing I didn't have.

And that was: The time I'd missed out on.

SEEKING TO FILL THE HOLE

The emotions that drove me as a child, as a teenager, and as a young man to find my family also drove me to achieve many great and nearly-impossible accomplishments in my life.

Being driven to reunite with my family taught me to persevere, to persist, to endure no matter what obstacles lay in my path. That obsession taught me to push, push, push, to make something of my life that would make my family proud. I'm certain that motivation to excel, to achieve my goals, was instrumental in helping me find them.

SHADOWS OF EMOTIONS

But still, I wonder.

Why were all those "Why?" questions so important to me?

Why did I have this obsession with knowing the answers?

I'll tell you why: Because the answers gave me a sense of belonging. A sense of identity. A sense of "I know who I am, I know where I come from, I know who I look like, I know why I'm shy, why I'm gentle, why I'm angry, why I'm aggressive."

Most adoptees, and most folks in foster care, live their lives seeking those answers. It's part of being human—wanting and yearning for connection. As an adult now, and as a father, I also have a yearning to pass this information on to my own kids, to help them feel complete, not disconnected and disowned as I'd felt.

Seeking the answers never stops.

Finding the answers only brings new questions. New holes to fill.

KEVIN IJA BARNETT, SR.

With my mom's passing, the holes to fill seem even deeper and wider. Some days, the holes feel bottomless.

There remain so many "Why?" questions now that will never be answered, that can never even be asked. In the three years, I was blessed with my mom, we created so many beautiful memories. Yet it's the holes in my past that haunt me. I have come to realize that not having all the answers is part of my journey—and accepting that fact is perhaps the next phase of the journey.

Trust me, accepting that reality is hard. It brings up a lot of anger. Finding ways to channel that anger can be a daily struggle—it feels easier to let myself dwell in anger than to seek peace. I deal with those feelings by logging onto my Facebook group, by listening to music, by just getting out of the house and going for a ride. And I channel that anxiety and angst by writing these books, by speaking publicly about my story and helping to heal others.

Now that my mother and father are both gone, learning to appreciate what time I was blessed with is crucial to my well-being. I'm grateful for the challenges I faced and overcame, during the process of searching for my family—without that, I wouldn't be who I am today. That journey shaped me.

ACCEPTING THE QUESTIONS WITHOUT ANSWERS

Even with the answers to some of my questions, accepting who I am has remained a struggle. At times, I still feel broken.

Opening myself to accepting the truth about my journey has helped me heal some of those broken parts of me.

If I were going to speak to parents, like my adopted mom and dad, who had not opened themselves to sharing the truth with their adopted children, here's what I'd say:

KEVIN IJA BARNETT, SR.

These children will deal with many types of internal emotions their entire lives—emotions they cannot explain. They will suffer from depression. They will suffer unexplained anxiety and issues with control. They will bottle up and hold onto a lot of untapped anger. One day, they might act out on that anger.

This anger isn't healthy. All children should know who they are. And where they come from.

But how should these parents bridge that gap, to reconcile and heal the emotions these children are feeling?

Two words:

Be honest.

Be honest, and let them know who they are. And where they come from.

Take them to Social Services. Help them find their medical records. Give them as much information as you possibly can about themselves—find their original birth certificates, for example. Don't hide anything.

SHADOWS OF EMOTIONS

You can replace their biological mother and father by doing mother and father things together. But you cannot replace that inner bond they will never have with their birth parents, with their bloodline.

Don't lie to them about their birthright. You'd be doing an injustice to them, by lying.

What would I say to people like you and me, who are still searching for their biological parents? What would I say to those of you who haven't yet made the leap to searching, but still have those lingering "Why?" questions replaying in your head?

Find your parents.

Find your bloodline.

Find the answers.

Because if you have that desire to know, to understand, to feel closure, to find connection, that itch is never going to go away.

Don't struggle all your life with the questions.

Do something.

Take action.

If you're not taking action, if you're not seeking to fill that hole in your life, you are always going to have the questions and no answers.

Take action.

And if your actions bring answers you can't handle?

Then let it go. You've done all you can. Fill the hole in your life by seeking the comfort and emotional support of those around you—those folks who know the true you, who accept you because of who you are, with those who sustain you in your times of need.

And with those who truly love you.

Which brings me to the next subject in *Shadows of Emotions*: The emotion called love.

CHAPTER TEN

Love

Our journey to define, decipher and interpret our feelings in *Shadows of Emotions* comes at last to the emotion that drives the creation of more songs, more books, more movies and more demonstrations of intense emotion than any other.

It's the emotion called love.

Love is without a doubt the most difficult emotion of all to define. It's nearly impossible to explain in words. It defies easy categorization, it changes its meaning depending upon the circumstances and the people involved, and yet it's an emotion we all can identify when we feel it.

Ask ten people to define love, and you'll receive ten different definitions.

Love is a gift.

Love is a miracle.

Love hurts.

Love heals.

Love protects.

Love sacrifices.

Love saves.

This thing called love is truly a mystery, an enigma even science cannot explain.

You cannot touch it, but you can feel it.

You cannot see it, but you can see its work in your life.

You cannot hear it, but you can express love in words.

Even under the direst of circumstances, even during our worst trauma and tragedy, we can see signs of love at work all around us.

Love is the emotion each and every one of us craves, from the cradle to the grave. We

SHADOWS OF EMOTIONS

each need love for our well-being, for our emotional health, for our purpose, and for our survival.

According to the ancient Greeks, there are 8 different kinds of love:

agape—unconditional love.

Eros—romantic love.

Philia—affectionate love.

Philautia—self-love.

Storge—family love.

Ludus—playful love.

mania—obsessive love.

Our lives are driven by love. And yet this emotion called love remains an unsolved mystery to most of us—elusive, evasive, intangible, inexpressible. Without love, we struggle with feelings of worthlessness, our lives hollow and empty, our hopes and dreams purposeless.

Feeling unloved might be the worst emotion a human can feel.

Yet for adoptees, for children who were orphaned or abandoned, and for those placed in foster care, that's often the first emotion that comes to mind. That feeling of being abandoned, discarded, disposable and cast aside by our own family often rules our lives and controls our future.

So how does love fit into our journey? That's the question I want to answer in this chapter.

THE INSTILLING OF LOVE

When I learned the reasons my birth mother gave me up, it took a while for me to realize her decision was based upon love. Her #1 priority was her maternal love for me.

My mother didn't have the proper resources, or the emotional support and maturity she felt she needed, to take care of me. Out of love, she gave me up, surrendering me in the hopes of a better life for her newborn son, believing another family would raise me, protect me, and love me.

Surrendering me was her way of imprinting her love on me. It was out of a desire to instill love that I was placed in the foster care system.

Once I was removed from the foster care system, and into my adopted family, the Barnett family, it was there that the true meaning of love was revealed to me.

The Barnetts instilled me with love. They showed me love from the first day I came into their lives. They sacrificed, to give me a loving home. Because of their love, it allowed me to comprehend what love really means, to let go of some of my childhood rage and anger. Their love helped me deal with my childhood issues of abandonment. Their love continues to teach me and heal me even now, as an adult.

Their unconditional love also helped me during the times I sought to forgive my birth mom, for what she'd done to me. My animosity and unforgiveness slowly vanished, because of the love the Barnetts instilled in me.

It was this teaching by the Barnetts that allowed me to forgive my mom on her deathbed, to show no regrets about the past, and to openly express to her how much I loved her. In fact, my last words to her were words of forgiveness and love, and her final words to me were, "I love you too, son."

Because of the Barnetts' support, because I was raised in a house filled with love, I became a product of love. That love they poured into me became the foundation for who I would become, for the man I am. Never did they refer to me as "their adopted son." I never heard that once. Instead, it was always "That's our son."

Things were much different in the Crawfords' home, in my first home in the foster care system.

SHADOWS OF EMOTIONS

THE DEATH OF LOVE

Raised in the Crawford family home, I never once experienced a feeling of love. Not once. Instead, my life with the Crawfords was filled with hatred, with anger, with violence, with terror, with abuse. I couldn't wait until I left that house. When Mr. Crawford, my foster father, finally died, I cracked. The negative and vengeful emotions I'd bottled up all those years caught up, and overwhelmed me.

Love never had a chance to prosper and grow there. Love died there.

The closest thing to love I recall from the Crawford household was toward the end of my time there. When Mrs. Crawford was dying, when she was about to leave this Earth, I needed to release my rage, the toxic hold my past held on me, and to tell her, "I forgive you." I forgave her, for all the pain, suffering and sorrow, because I needed to forgive myself. In order for me to live, in order for me to go on with my life, in order to grow and survive, I had to release all that anger and hatred they'd instilled in me.

In order to save my own soul, I forgave her.

I didn't even attend her funeral. By that time, I was numb from all the years of abuse. In my mind, I'd moved on. My emotions were deadened. I had no feelings—not anger, not sadness, not regret. Not even relief at being freed by her death had survived my time at the Crawfords. They'd trampled on all the good feelings every normal child should experience and killed them.

The miracle is that one emotion survived that trauma, though for years it remained buried deep in my heart. I was able to unearth it later in life when I discovered the sacrifice my birth mom had made on my behalf, and the strength it took to make that sacrifice, trusting in some Higher Power that everything would be all right.

That's the miracle of love.

SHADOWS OF EMOTIONS

THE MIRACLE OF LOVE

But what kind of love is that—that sacrificial love one person makes to save another?

It took years for me to understand that kind of love—the love my birth mom exhibited when she gave me away to a new home.

Think about it. Think about the emotional toll it took on any woman, back then in the 1960s, to give her baby away to the State, because she couldn't afford the care that baby might need because she wanted a life for that baby she couldn't provide.

My birth mom could have aborted me. That was a choice she could have made.

But she didn't.

She could have thrown me in the garbage can.

But she didn't.

Instead, she went through the painstaking process of giving me birth, giving me life, and giving me a good home—better than the home she could provide, she hoped. Afterward, she continued to fund my existence by sending money to the State and helping out financially whenever she could.

It was only later in life that I learned this. I found out money was being sent to the State for me, while I was still in foster care. That fact tells me my mother loved me and wanted nothing but the best for me. Though I still had qualms about why she never reached out and contacted me—she was probably embarrassed, I'd guess—I understood that it took love to do that.

It took unconditional love. It took faith. And it took strength. I truly don't know if I could have given one of my children away.

That's one of the divine miracles of love. It gives us the strength and courage to do the impossible.

Reaching out and contacting my birth family took a little of that same courage. I didn't know whether to expect that they'd accept me, much less love me.

I went into it expecting nothing. At best, I figured my chances of being embraced and welcomed into the family were 50-50. If I wasn't accepted, if I didn't receive their love, I wasn't going to stress—I vowed to be proud of reaching my goal and finding my family. I took the next step on my journey hoping for the best, praying for a miracle.

The miracle of it all is that the love I felt from them was instant.

It was instant love, from day one.

From day one, I felt wanted. I felt accepted. The Barnetts had instilled that same loving acceptance in me, during my childhood and teenage years. Meeting my birth family, I instantly felt their love pour out on me. They didn't turn me away or disown me. There was no hesitation. My birth mom, my sister, my brother, and cousins—they all wanted me in their lives.

Through love, we bonded.

Through love, the past no longer felt painful.

Through love, our future together looked hopeful.

Through love, I experienced the joy and happiness I'd always dreamed of.

Through love, I healed.

That instant love felt like Christmas morning coming in September! No other words can express my emotions so well. It was like that feeling as a child, waiting 12 long months for Christmas Day to roll around. Waiting and waiting and waiting! And then when the day comes, and you crawl out of bed and go look under the Christmas tree, and see a gift with your name on it—it's that feeling of intense joy, that playful, giddy feeling where you cry on the inside and laugh on the outside as you race to the tree and unwrap your present.

On Christmas Day, love and joy flow everywhere. Christmas Day makes all the bad

SHADOWS OF EMOTIONS

days go away. Bad times are forgotten, put aside for one glorious day.

Only love has that power. Only love can redeem the past. Only love can be broken into pieces, shattered and splintered, and then restored. Of all the emotions we've talked about, only love has the power to transform, to renew relationships, to change lives, to save lives.

Love heals.

Love protects.

Love sacrifices.

And, love forgives.

Love erases all the negative emotional shadows. Love gives us a clear vision of life that reflects our deepest dreams.

Which brings us now to our next chapter, and the emotion with the deepest ties to the past. That's the emotion called regret.

CHAPTER ELEVEN

Regret

As we near the end of our journey to explore the shadow of emotions, seeking to understand how they consciously and subconsciously affect each and every one of us, we come at last to one of the most heartbreaking emotions of all.

Regret.

Now I know what you're probably thinking to yourself.

Regret? Why do I have to think about my regrets? All the times and places I've pained, punished and negatively impacted others in my life? And all the times I've let myself and others down? All the dreams I abandoned? All the things I wish I'd done differently?

Why do we need to dig into the past, to change my future?

LIVING IN THE PAST

Regret is an emotion that lives in the past. Regret hounds and haunts us about our past mistakes, our past failures, our under-achievements, and our life's greatest disappointments.

Regret hits, batters and bombards us from both the past and the future, crushing our hopes from every angle.

Regret is like a two-sided coin. One side is the future; the other side, the past. There is always a flip-side to regret—if we regret one event or one action in our life, it forces us to lose hope that we can do better in the future. It colors and shadows our ability to heal, to forgive ourselves. Instead of appreciating the lesson we've learned from stumbling and falling, we focus instead on the probability that we'll stumble and fall again.

And again.

And again.

Regret spins in our head. Regret focuses on the curse, instead of the blessing.

Let me use my own life as an example.

If I had lived a normal life—if I'd been born and raised by my birth mother, instead of abandoned, raised in a foster home and adopted—I never would have known anything about the Barnett family, and wouldn't have lived the life I have now.

The Barnetts raised me with love. They positioned me to be successful. Because I was raised in the church, I had a moral compass to follow. I'll never know if that would have happened with my natural family—it could have, but the truth is I'll never know. Maybe I wouldn't have joined the military; maybe instead, I'd have grown up in the streets, and become a criminal, or a drug dealer.

KEVIN IJA BARNETT, SR.

There's no doubt my life would have turned out different.

Even with being raised in a loving household, with a roof over my head and all my wants and needs fulfilled, and with all I've overcome and accomplished as an adult, I still regret a lot of things.

I regret not meeting my brother earlier— I regret that immensely. It stems from the choices my mother made. I regret that my big brother had to go through his entire life being the male in the house—especially when my mother got up in age. He had to be there, always. He took on the father role because my mother's husband passed away.

I could see the pain in my brother's eyes, the first day we met. It was like a sigh of relief, that he finally had another male figure in the family, to carry some of the load.

I regret that he had to go through that pain and carry that burden all alone.

SHADOWS OF EMOTIONS

I also regret that I had no relationship with my father—not a hug, not even an "I'm so proud of you, son." Not anything. He might not have known I even existed, up until a certain point.

My father died alone. I regret that deeply, the man passed away with nobody at his bedside, dying in a chair in his apartment.

I regret never meeting a single one of my uncles, my grandfather, or my grandmother. My grandmother on my father's side actually passed a year after I was born. That hurts. My grandmother on my mother's side passed while I was graduating from college, so we never met.

The regrets keep coming and coming.

I regret not growing up with my sisters Gwen and Victoria on my father's side. We've bonded now that we're adults, but the bond could be so much closer if we'd been raised together. I wish I would have been more in her son's life, my nephew's life, and help to be a positive male role model.

That's just the family side.

Perhaps my deeper regrets lie in my dark past when I was trapped in the foster care system. Being dragged through all the physical, mental and sexual emotions that the Crawfords bludgeoned my childhood with. I regret that my foster brother is now in jail—I wish I'd been around to prevent that. I feel I should have been more of a presence in his life.

When I think about my birth story, the regrets start piling up. I regret the way I was born, the way I was abandoned and left for dead, the life that was handed to me in the beginning. Like I've said before, everything happens for a reason. So if the coin was flipped to the other side, if I'd lived a "normal" life, would I be able to sit here writing my book? Writing a book would have been the furthest thing from my mind! I probably would have skipped the military, college, and obtaining my degree.

SHADOWS OF EMOTIONS

Certainly, my emotional make-up would have been different.

Because of my circumstances, because of the situations I was raised in, and because of all I've overcome, I have a deep sense of pride in who I am. Pride is what pushes me to the limit to succeed. I doubt I'd have felt that same push, that same motivation to succeed, if I had been raised in a "normal" situation, and lived a "normal" life.

My whole life would be different.

It could have been better.

And it could have been worse.

And for that, I am undyingly thankful.

Being thankful for the life I have doesn't take away the regrets. Regret is always there, whispering in my ear, screaming in my mind about something.

As far as my birth mom, since her passing, there are new regrets. Now all I have of our relationship are memories and photographs. Same for my father. I have photos—one photo he even hung over his bed. When I touch that picture, I feel my father, realizing his hand also touched it.

I appreciate that connection, as slender as it is. I appreciate that I can look at my 102-year-old aunt, knowing she knows who I am, knowing I love her. I can look at my cousins, and know the same emotions and connections that exist between us.

The idea behind writing this book came to me to help connect others with their bloodline, to help heal the disconnection people feel. Healing regret isn't easy.

But trust me, as painful as regret is, there's a way out.

THE REALITY OF REGRET

First of all, let's define regret.

Regret is like the game show, Let's Make A Deal. You pick door number three, and it's a vacation to Cancun. Great! Until you find out that behind door number one was your dream car. You received a great gift, but you didn't get the gift of your dreams. You regret that you didn't pick door number one. So you saddle the gift you've been given with dissatisfaction, with unhappiness, with negative emotions, negative reactions. You don't realize that you could have picked door number two—behind which there was a bottle full of mud.

Your emotions are jumbled, out of control. You're happy, you're regretful, and you're dissatisfied, all at the same time.

Your emotions are all bottled up in that regret—in your inability to accept the way things turned out.

Dissatisfied with the way one thing turned out, you turn that dissatisfaction into regret about your whole life—every single bad choice you've ever made. You think I've messed up again. Everybody else gets all the good breaks. I wish I wasn't so stupid. I wish my life would have turned out differently.

We all feel regret at some point in our lives. We wish we'd acted differently, chosen differently, thought differently. That's just being human. That's just the reality of life.

HEALING FROM REGRET

Since my birth mom passed, I've pondered the meaning of regret. I've pondered its purpose. And I've pondered if my mom had her own regrets.

I know she went to her grave holding a lot of secrets. There were many things we never found the time or place to talk about—and other things I know she would have hidden no matter how many years together we had. Did she have regrets about our relationship? About abandoning me to foster care?

Although I'll never know the truth, the one thing I do know is this: She did her best, considering the circumstances. She even told her caregiver this, before she passed away. "Listen," she said, "I did the best I could. I just wanted the best for him. And he turned out okay."

Had she the opportunity to do it all over again, she probably would have done things differently. She saw the pain I'd experienced. That pain hurt her deeply. She suffered herself, in keeping her secrets; for years, she pushed her mind to believe that I didn't exist.

Her regrets ran deep. So did the regrets of others in my family.

My sister Anna expressed this to me once. "I wish you'd been with me from our youth," she told me. "We would have really been close."

Hearing those words, I'm bombarded by every emotion imaginable. My regret makes me feel selfish. Because I feel selfish, I become angry. Anger is a feeling I find hard to shake. When I'm angry, I stop communicating with everybody.

To combat my anger and regret, I change my mindset. I try to think positive. I'll look at a photo of my family, of my children, to remind me of positive things, of the people I love and those who love me. Feeling those positive emotions brings me out of my negative mood.

Sometimes I hear my mother's voice in my head. I feel my mom subconsciously speaking to me, and that snaps me out of my regrets.

Having something positive to turn to, to hold onto, is the key. Focus in on that positive thought, that positive memory. Allow the feelings of regret to move through you—don't try to hold them back, or bottle them up. Don't fight them. Allow them to flow through and be released.

Accept your regrets.

Then learn how to control them, to steer them in a positive way.

Remember: No situation is all bad. Not mine. Not yours.

SHADOWS OF EMOTIONS

When something bad happens, seek out the positivity in it. Don't run from regret. Don't hide from it.

Accept it. Deal with it. Then release it.

Find your own personal mechanism of acceptance and control. It's useful for all emotions—regret, anger, denial, sorrow, hate, depression. Regret can be controlled and dealt with—we all experience it, all the way from childhood to old age, and every stage of life in-between.

Living in regret can be destructive.

Living in the past robs you of your future.

Ask yourself: What regret are you holding onto? What regret is keeping you chained and caged to a past failure?

Seek it out, accept it, deal with it, and release it. And you can claw your way out of that cage, one regret at a time.

At this stage in the book, we've spoken about nearly every emotion imaginable: anger, guilt, depression, joy, hope, rejection, peace, love, and regret.

It's time for our journey to come full-circle. It's time to face the final shadows you and I live in. Time to step into those shadows, and be released once and forever from our bondage.

CHAPTER TWELVE

Released From the Shadows

In my first book, *Living My Shadows: Dreams Do Come True*, the final chapter was titled "Shadows Disappearing at the Light of Day." I wrapped up my first book by sharing all the scars and pain I'd overcome in the past, and how I'd used those scars to fuel my journey, to make myself stronger.

My journey in writing the first book was to inspire others—like you—to have the courage to take that same journey. To find your missing family members—no matter what cruel circumstances might await you, without allowing fear, depression or anxiety to stop you.

KEVIN IJA BARNETT, SR.

My journey in writing my second book, *Shadows of Emotions*, was to understand those emotions we all face on that journey. To face, battle and defeat the negative emotions, and turn that struggle into the weapons of triumph, of reaching our personal dreams.

When I think back to where my life started, and where my life is now, I'm overwhelmed. Overwhelmed with wonder. Overwhelmed with gratitude. Overwhelmed with questions. Overwhelmed with the answers I never thought I'd receive.

Reaching out to help other people who've walked my same walk was never my dream or ambition, as a young child in foster care. Yet that is the walk I have walked.

Through facing the hardships in life head-on, I experienced a dramatic turnaround in my circumstances.

I became able to handle any emotion. Don't get me wrong–the negative emotions didn't disappear. They didn't stop coming. But

SHADOWS OF EMOTIONS

hardship taught me to accept them, to deal with them, to control them, and then to release them.

To use my negative emotions to heal and strengthen myself.

I came out of the foster care system pretty well—better than most. My journey allowed me to share my first-hand experiences of hardships with others, and to speak from a place of pain and hard truths.

I became successful by overcoming obstacles, no matter how difficult they seemed.

Do I know why I was chosen for this life? I have no idea why. I do know that if I had my life to live all over again, I would change a few things.

I would have pressed harder, to find my family faster.

I would have dug deeper, and connected on a more intimate level with my birth mom, in the time we had together.

KEVIN IJA BARNETT, SR.

I would have been more engaging with my daughter, more open to learning what she was going through in life.

The flip-side of that is that if I hadn't experienced these things, I wouldn't be as understanding, as strong, as motivated as I am. I never would have learned the benefit of persevering, or how to make something positive out of negativity.

Without my hardships, I never would have learned to appreciate what I have—materialistically, financially, spiritually.

My hardships taught me toughness. My struggles gave me fortitude. My battles drilled me in clarity of purpose.

Now that I've found my birth family, I appreciate every little thing, whether positive or negative. I know how fortunate and wholly blessed I am—there are so many out there who still don't know who their birth parents are. I lived with that dual-identity of questioning-and-not-knowing who I am for 56 years.

SHADOWS OF EMOTIONS

I know what the shadows look like. I decided if I couldn't creep out of them, I'd stand tall in the shadows, and I'd dance.

Dancing in the shadows is me telling my story.

Overall, I'm thankful to even be in a position to tell it.

Now I want to help you tell your story. To take your own journey.

But how? How can I help you stay motivated, inspired to overcome all the roadblocks? The dead ends? The obstacles?

Here's how:

Think about the prize waiting for you on the other end.

The prize is the culmination of your dream. The prize is the blood connection you seek. The prize is finally having the answer to the question: Who am I?

The prize is living a happy, fulfilled life. The prize is learning you truly are somebody.

Not nobody.

Don't believe that lie for a moment. Don't give the negative voices in your head an excuse for you not to succeed. Use that negativity and all life's obstacles as fuel for the fire.

Every little obstacle, every piece of negativity, is a brick. A brick toward building your dream house. Take those bricks and one brick at a time start building your house. Keep building, until you build yourself a mansion of success.

Find your own vehicle to help you stay focused, and stay in your lane.

If you can do that, you can become anything you want.

I'm living proof that you can become anything, achieve anything. But you must be willing to sacrifice. You must be willing to give, and to change course, when needed. To be flexible. To fail, and use that failure as your motivator.

SHADOWS OF EMOTIONS

Never, never, ever give up. Once you give up, that's it. It's the end of the story. You're hidden forever in the shadows. There's no escape, no release.

In many ways, I'm still living in my shadows. There remain so many questions I haven't answered. Family, I haven't met. Family, I'll never meet.

I'm still living in the shadows of not knowing.

That truth is hard to accept. Maybe I'll never be completely out of the shadows. I can't make up for the first 56 years of my life. I'll never catch up on all I missed—my father, my grandfather, my grandmother on my father's side—the list goes on and on and on.

I still have anger. I still feel hatred. At times I still find myself trapped in a whirlwind of negative emotional moods, in pessimism, in defeatism. And I still ask God, "Why?"

All that is part of living in a shadow. But that's why this book is called Life After the

Dream. Because after the dream, there's still everyday life to deal with, everyday emotions to combat, everyday ups-and-downs to struggle against.

I may be in my shadows for the rest of my life. But I am no longer controlled by those shadows. I'm no longer at the mercy of those storms of emotion. I'm no longer drowning in a sea of negativity.

Beginning your own journey will part those stormy seas, and open the emotional floodgates. That's a natural reaction. Once the waters start pouring in, prepare yourself mentally and spiritually for all the hidden aspects of finding and being reunited with your family.

You must become a master of your emotions, to take the journey, to ride the emotional rollercoaster all the way to its final destination: the realization of your deepest dream.

SHADOWS OF EMOTIONS

If you're ready to take that ride, I congratulate you! It's time.

Rise up.

Focus on your dream.

Be bold. March forward.

Keep your head and your hopes up.

Make no excuses.

Rewrite the narrative for your life.

Find your bloodline.

Celebrate your healing.

Share your story.

And don't let your happy ending go untold. Others need to see that light of hope shining in the darkness.

I hope this book has been that light shining in the darkness for you. If it has, pass that light on.

Take care. Live your dream. And God bless you.

IN GRATITUDE

I would like to thank both mothers for helping me be the man that I am.

Lois, thank you for bringing me into this world. I can only imagine how hard it was to give me up at birth, but now I understand and know why. If it wasn't for that act, who knows where I would be today.

Muriel, I thank you for accepting me and giving me the opportunity to be who I am today. Because of the discipline and always wanting my siblings and me to be the best that we could be, I am truly living the dream. You are my hero.

KEVIN IJA BARNETT, SR.

Lois & Muriel, R.I.P
Your son,
Kevin

Special thanks to my wife Sharon F. Pelham, for putting up with all the craziness that she had to endure during the process of writing this book.

For my children:
Kevin J Barnett, Jr.
Isaiah J. Barnett
Patrice Daniels
Charles B.C.D. Boling
Darrius J. Barnett

For my stepdaughter,
Samantha L. Justice (photographer)

SHADOWS OF EMOTIONS

For my grandchildren:

Saniah

Iquan

Kevin

Isaiah

Zuri

Ki'Re

Kayla

Mekhi

CONTACT

I'm passionate about sharing my story with an interactive Author Talk at libraries, and for community groups. Along with reading passages from *Shadows of Emotions: Life After The Dream*, I pose questions to the group and answer questions from the audience. I'll discuss my journey through the foster care and adoption system and the strength and confidence I found in the military. It concludes with the trials and triumphs of finding my birth parents and extended family.

The story will resonate with those who have been part of the foster care/adoption system, or those looking for a deeper understanding of the impact on children. It will also resonate with those who want to connect more deeply with their roots, and with anyone needing to feel inspired to follow their heart.

If you are interested in learning more, please visit my website:

www.livingmyshadows.org

Or contact my foundation:

LivingMyShadows, LLC
560 Peoples Plaza, #290
Newark, DE. 19702
PHONE: (302) 353-9841
EMAIL: livingmyshadows@gmail.com

ABOUT THE AUTHOR

Kevin I.J.A. Barnett, Sr is a Retired Non-Commissioned Officer of the United States Army. He has served in Germany, Afghanistan, and many stateside tours during his career. He is married to Sharon F. Pelham and does Author Talks and book signings when time permits.

www.ingramcontent.com/pod-product-compliance
Lightning Source LLC
Chambersburg PA
CBHW071359290426
44108CB00014B/1612